Meal Salads

Jean Paré

www.companyscoming.com
visit our website

Front Cover

1. West Coast Salmon Salad, page 92

Back Cover

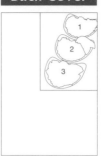

1. Persian Rice Salad, page 100
2. Russian Wild Rice Salad, page 97
3. Berry Brie Salad, page 39

Props: Hutschenreuther

Meal Salads

Copyright © Company's Coming Publishing Limited

All rights reserved worldwide. No part of this book may be reproduced, stored in a retrieval system or transmitted in any form by any means without written permission in advance from the publisher.

In the case of photocopying or other reprographic copying, a license may be purchased from the Canadian Copyright Licensing Agency (Access Copyright). Visit www.accesscopyright.ca or call toll free 1-800-893-5777. In the United States, please contact the Copyright Clearance Centre at www.copyright.com or call 978-646-8600.

Brief portions of this book may be reproduced for review purposes, provided credit is given to the source. Reviewers are invited to contact the publisher for additional information.

Fourth Printing March 2011

Library and Archives Canada Cataloguing in Publication

Paré, Jean, date-
Meal salads / Jean Paré.
(Original series) Includes index.
At head of title: Company's Coming.
ISBN 978-1-897477-30-4
1. Salads. I. Title. II. Series: Paré, Jean, date.
Original series.
TX740.P34819 2010   641.8'3   C2009-903040-3

Published by
Company's Coming Publishing Limited
2311 – 96 Street
Edmonton, Alberta, Canada T6N 1G3
Tel: 780-450-6223   Fax: 780-450-1857
www.companyscoming.com

Company's Coming is a registered trademark owned by Company's Coming Publishing Limited

We acknowledge the financial support of the Government of Canada through the Canada Book Fund for our publishing activities.

Printed in China

We gratefully acknowledge the following suppliers for their generous support of our Test and Photography Kitchens:

Broil King Barbecues
Corelle®
Hamilton Beach® Canada
Lagostina®
Proctor Silex® Canada
Tupperware®

Our special thanks to the following business for providing props for photography:

Stokes

Get more great recipes...FREE!

click

search

print

cook

From apple pie to zucchini bread, we've got you covered. Browse our free online recipes for Guaranteed Great!™ results.

You can also sign up to receive our **FREE online newsletter**. You'll receive exclusive offers, FREE recipes & cooking tips, new title previews, and much more...all delivered to your in-box.

So don't delay, visit our website today!

www.companyscoming.com
visit our ↑ website

Company's Coming Cookbooks

Quick & easy recipes; everyday ingredients!

Original Series

- Softcover, 160 pages
- Lay-flat plastic comb binding
- Full-colour photos
- Nutrition information

Original Series

- Softcover, 160 pages
- Lay-flat plastic comb binding
- Full-colour photos
- Nutrition information

2-in-1 Cookbook Collection

- Softcover, 256 pages
- Lay-flat plastic coil binding
- Full-colour photos
- Nutrition information

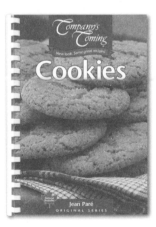

Original Series

- Softcover, 160 pages
- Lay-flat plastic comb binding
- Full-colour photos
- Updated format

For a complete listing of our cookbooks, visit our website:
www.companyscoming.com

Table of Contents

Leafy Greens

Fruit

Pasta &
Noodles

Legumes &
Grains

Slaws &
Vegetables

The Company's Coming Story

Jean Paré (pronounced "jeen PAIR-ee") grew up understanding that the combination of family, friends and home cooking is the best recipe for a good life. From her mother, she learned to appreciate good cooking, while her father praised even her earliest attempts in the kitchen. When Jean left home, she took with her a love of cooking, many family recipes and an intriguing desire to read cookbooks as if they were novels!

"Never share a recipe you wouldn't use yourself."

When her four children had all reached school age, Jean volunteered to cater the 50th anniversary celebration of the Vermilion School of Agriculture, now Lakeland College, in Alberta, Canada. Working out of her home, Jean prepared a dinner for more than 1,000 people, launching a flourishing catering operation that continued for over 18 years. During that time, she had countless opportunities to test new ideas with immediate feedback—resulting in empty plates and contented customers! Whether preparing cocktail sandwiches for a house party or serving a hot meal for 1,500 people, Jean Paré earned a reputation for great food, courteous service and reasonable prices.

As requests for her recipes increased, Jean was often asked the question, "Why don't you write a cookbook?" Jean responded by teaming up with her son, Grant Lovig, in the fall of 1980 to form Company's Coming Publishing Limited. The publication of *150 Delicious Squares* on April 14, 1981 marked the debut of what would soon become one of the world's most popular cookbook series.

The company has grown since those early days when Jean worked from a spare bedroom in her home. Today, she continues to write recipes while working closely with the staff of the Recipe Factory, as the Company's Coming test kitchen is affectionately known.

There she fills the role of mentor, assisting with the development of recipes people most want to use for everyday cooking and easy entertaining. Every Company's Coming recipe is *kitchen-tested* before it is approved for publication.

Jean's daughter, Gail Lovig, is responsible for marketing and distribution, leading a team that includes sales personnel located in major cities across Canada. Company's Coming cookbooks are distributed in Canada, the United States, Australia and other world markets. Bestsellers many times over in English, Company's Coming cookbooks have also been published in French and Spanish.

Familiar and trusted in home kitchens around the world, Company's Coming cookbooks are offered in a variety of formats. Highly regarded as kitchen workbooks, the softcover Original Series, with its lay-flat plastic comb binding, is still a favourite among readers.

Jean Paré's approach to cooking has always called for *quick and easy recipes* using *everyday ingredients*. That view has served her well. The recipient of many awards, including the Queen Elizabeth Golden Jubilee Medal, Jean was appointed Member of the Order of Canada, her country's highest lifetime achievement honour.

Jean continues to gain new supporters by adhering to what she calls The Golden Rule of Cooking: *Never share a recipe you wouldn't use yourself.* It's an approach that has worked—*millions of times over!*

Foreword

Salads have long been beloved for their variety, colour and versatility—a crisp garden starter or a light lunch of pasta salad is often just the thing. Meal salads take it one step further, providing at least one source of protein—and since most contain vegetables or fruit, they're packing an array of nutrients, too! Entree salads are more popular than ever, creating lighter meal options that don't sacrifice flavour for nutrition. That's where *Meal Salads* comes in. We've created a recipe collection with delicious salads for every meal of the day, including breakfast! What a unique way to serve a balanced menu.

The word "salad" may be synonymous with greens, but making it a meal means so much more! *Meal Salads* has it covered with delightful fruit salads, wholesome grains and legumes, creamy pasta and noodle salads, crisp slaws, layered salads and (we couldn't leave them out!) leafy greens. Don't feel the need to follow every recipe to the letter—if you have a different type of lettuce, for example, feel free to use it. See for yourself how easy it is to experiment with ingredients you have on hand.

The simplicity of most entree salads makes them perfect for weekday meal solutions, while convenient hand-held options such as Satay Chicken Salad Wraps are perfect for packed lunches. Elegant offerings such as Blue Cheese Tenderloin Salad make for easy entertaining. And don't forget about picnics and potlucks! With handy shortcuts such as packaged mixed greens, precut veggies and bottled dressings, you can prepare a fabulous meal salad in no time!

Meal Salads is chock full of fresh, light recipes to bring nutritional balance and variety to your meals. With the diverse selection of ingredients we've included, chances are you'll end up trying something new, too! You and your family will thank us for it.

Jean Paré

Nutrition Information Guidelines

Each recipe is analyzed using the most current version of the Canadian Nutrient File from Health Canada, which is based on the United States Department of Agriculture (USDA) Nutrient Database.

- If more than one ingredient is listed (such as "butter or hard margarine"), or if a range is given (1 – 2 tsp., 5 – 10 mL), only the first ingredient or first amount is analyzed.

- For meat, poultry and fish, the serving size per person is based on the recommended 4 oz. (113 g) uncooked weight (without bone), which is 2 – 3 oz. (57 – 85 g) cooked weight (without bone)—approximately the size of a deck of playing cards.

- Milk used is 1% M.F. (milk fat), unless otherwise stated.

- Cooking oil used is canola oil, unless otherwise stated.

- Ingredients indicating "sprinkle," "optional," or "for garnish" are not included in the nutrition information.

- The fat in recipes and combination foods can vary greatly depending on the sources and types of fats used in each specific ingredient. For these reasons, the amount of saturated, monounsaturated and polyunsaturated fats may not add up to the total fat content.

Vera C. Mazurak, Ph.D.
Nutritionist

What Makes a Salad a Meal?

We're all familiar with what makes a salad—in the most basic terms, a mix of bite-sized vegetables, fruit, pasta, beans or grains, tossed in dressing and served warm or cold. A meal salad simply adds protein, essential for packing in the nutrition of a complete meal.

Every recipe in this book contains a protein source, and we've used a variety to keep things interesting. Not only will you find tender meats and seafood, but also other healthful protein sources such as soybeans, lentils, eggs, quinoa and tofu. Some of the salads even include the full spectrum of food groups—talk about a well-rounded meal!

Preparing and Storing Meal Salads

Here are a few tips for preparing the best, most flavourful meal salads. Creating entree salads on your own may seem daunting, but putting them together can be a breeze— they can even be made with ingredients you likely already have on hand.

All About Ingredients

We believe that fresh ingredients make the most delicious salads—that's why, wherever possible, we've used fresh fruit, vegetables and herbs to maximize the flavour. It is important to ensure that all fresh produce is washed thoroughly, and then either patted dry with paper towel or spun dry in a salad spinner before being used. Some bagged mixed greens come washed and ready to use, making them a great shortcut ingredient. Many recipes will ask you to "julienne" ingredients—this means to slice them into thin strips that resemble matchsticks— making for a salad with a clean look and easy, fork-sized bites.

Keeping a few basic ingredients on hand makes throwing together a meal salad a snap. Of course, the base of a salad doesn't always have to be greens—for convenience and variety, try using other ingredients that store well for longer periods. Pasta, potatoes, grains, beans and rice are ideal pantry items to use in meal salads—some, such as beans, even double as a protein source.

Meat may be the first protein that comes to mind, but other healthy protein sources can also be kept on hand—your favourite nuts and cheeses are perfect for tossing into a salad to make it a meal. Some other pantry staples, such as dried fruit and seeds, provide great garnish possibilities too. Any fresh or frozen fruit or vegetable varieties you have, and even some canned ones, can be added for a colour and nutrition boost as well.

Substituting Ingredients

It is possible to substitute ingredients while preparing meal salads, but you'll need to decide which ingredients are crucial to a recipe's outcome, and which can be substituted. Think about what the ingredient contributes to the salad before choosing a substitution.

Be mindful that the ingredient you want to substitute should be similar in flavour to what's called for. If fresh strawberries provide sweet bites in a salad, you can usually get away with using almost any summer berry instead. On the other hand, if you use a bitter green such as radicchio in a salad that doesn't call for it, it may clash with other ingredients and upset the recipe's flavour balance.

Texture is also important to consider. If a pasta salad calls for spiraled rotini and you use radiatore, this short, ridged pasta will hold a creamy dressing in much the same way. If, however, you use a delicate leafy green in a salad with a thick dressing in place of a sturdier kind of lettuce such as romaine, it may not stand up to it and become wilted and soggy.

Dressing Basics

There are many options for dressing your meal salads. Use a from-scratch recipe from the following pages, a bottled dressing with your own flavour twist or a homemade vinaigrette. Creating a homemade dressing is much simpler than you might think! Basic vinaigrette is a combination of oil and vinegar—the traditional formula is three parts oil, such as olive or canola, to one part acid ingredient, such as vinegar or lemon juice. From this base, you can go as elaborate as you like by adding seasonings such as salt and pepper, garlic and fresh or dried herbs and spices—there are infinite combinations when it comes to personalizing your vinaigrette. To prevent homemade dressings and vinaigrettes from going rancid, they should be kept in the refrigerator and used within one week. Although olive and vegetable oils may harden when refrigerated, they return to liquid form when left at room temperature for a short time.

The recipes in this book will all yield salads with the appropriate ratio of main components to dressing. If you choose to use a bottled or homemade dressing as a substitute for the one in the recipe, use a light hand and add it a little bit at a time while gently tossing, until the salad is lightly coated. You can always add more, but too much dressing can ruin a salad, making it overly wet and drowning out the other flavours.

Storing Salads

Most salads are best eaten the day they are prepared. Anything made with greens, or other delicate ingredients that may become bogged down by dressing, will be at its peak for only the first few hours after it's made. Heavier, heartier salads such as pasta or potato salads can be kept for up to three days in the refrigerator.

When you need to take along a salad to be enjoyed later, whether it's being packed up for a lunch, picnic or potluck, a good rule of thumb is to keep "wet" and "dry" ingredients in separate containers. Store anything that could cause sogginess, such as chopped tomatoes or dressing, in separate containers. Toss the salad together just before serving.

Whatever salad you choose and wherever you enjoy it, a meal salad is a delicious choice for any time of the day.

Steak and Sweet Potato Salad

Toss your favourites on the grill to create this simple, appetizing salad!
A great meal for those hot summer days—no need for the oven.
Serve with garlic toast.

Fresh peeled orange-fleshed sweet potatoes, cut into 1/2 inch (12 mm) slices	1 lb.	454 g
Water	1 tbsp.	15 mL
Montreal steak spice	2 tsp.	10 mL
Beef strip loin steak	1 lb.	454 g
Fresh asparagus, trimmed of tough ends	1 lb.	454 g
Balsamic vinaigrette dressing	3 tbsp.	50 mL
Cut or torn romaine lettuce, lightly packed	6 cups	1.5 L
Halved cherry tomatoes	1 cup	250 mL
Balsamic vinaigrette dressing	1/3 cup	75 mL
Shaved Parmesan cheese	1/2 cup	125 mL

Arrange sweet potato slices in single layer on large microwave-safe plate. Sprinkle with water. Microwave, covered, on high (100%) for about 4 minutes until tender-crisp.

Sprinkle steak spice on both sides of steak. Preheat gas barbecue to medium-high. Cook steak on greased grill for about 4 minutes per side until internal temperature reaches 145°F (63°C) for medium-rare or until steak reaches desired doneness. Transfer to cutting board. Cover with foil. Let stand for 10 minutes. Slice thinly. Transfer to extra-large bowl.

Reduce heat to medium. Brush sweet potato and asparagus with first amount of dressing. Cook on greased grill for 8 to 10 minutes, turning occasionally, until browned and tender. Transfer to cutting board. Let stand until cool enough to handle. Cut into 1 inch (2.5 cm) pieces. Add to steak.

Add next 3 ingredients. Toss. Sprinkle with cheese. Makes about 14 cups (3.5 L).

1 1/2 cups (375 mL): 197 Calories; 8.5 g Total Fat (1.2 g Mono, 0.2 g Poly, 2.9 g Sat); 28 mg Cholesterol; 15 g Carbohydrate; 3 g Fibre; 15 g Protein; 426 mg Sodium

Steak Caesar Salad

Enjoy tender steak strips and a rich Caesar dressing with hints of garlic and citrus. Grilled sourdough croutons give this made-over classic an appealing look.

Beef rib-eye steak	1 lb.	454 g
Montreal steak spice	2 tsp.	10 mL
Egg yolk (large), see Safety Tip, next page	1	1
Lemon juice	2 tbsp.	30 mL
Capers, chopped (optional)	1 tbsp.	15 mL
Dijon mustard	1 tbsp.	15 mL
Salt	1/2 tsp.	2 mL
Coarsely ground pepper	1/2 tsp.	2 mL
Garlic cloves, chopped	2	2
(or 1/2 tsp., 2 mL, powder)		
Dried crushed chilies	1/4 tsp.	1 mL
Olive (or cooking) oil	1/3 cup	75 mL
Sourdough bread slices	2	2
Cut or torn romaine lettuce, lightly packed	8 cups	2 L
Grated Parmesan cheese	1/4 cup	60 mL

Sprinkle both sides of steak with steak spice. Preheat gas barbecue to medium-high. Cook steak on greased grill for about 4 minutes per side until internal temperature reaches 145°F (63°C) for medium-rare or until steak reaches desired doneness. Transfer to cutting board. Cover with foil. Let stand for 10 minutes. Slice thinly. Transfer to extra-large bowl.

Process next 8 ingredients in blender until combined. With motor running, add olive oil in thin stream through hole in lid until smooth.

Brush about 2 tbsp. (30 mL) olive oil mixture onto bread slices. Cook bread on greased grill for about 1 minute per side until grill marks appear. Transfer to cutting board. Let stand until cool enough to handle. Cut into 1 inch (2.5 cm) pieces. Add to steak.

Add lettuce and remaining olive oil mixture. Toss. Sprinkle with cheese. Makes about 12 cups (3 L).

1 1/2 cups (375 mL): 226 Calories; 14.6 g Total Fat (8.3 g Mono, 1.7 g Poly, 3.6 g Sat); 60 mg Cholesterol; 11 g Carbohydrate; 2 g Fibre; 14 g Protein; 506 mg Sodium

(continued on next page)

Safety Tip: This recipe contains uncooked egg. Make sure to use fresh, clean Grade A eggs. Keep chilled and consume the same day the recipe is prepared. Always discard leftovers. Pregnant women, young children and the elderly are not advised to eat anything containing raw egg.

Hacienda Salad

This family-friendly taco salad boasts crisp veggies and creamy avocado—a real crowd-pleaser! Serve with tortilla chips on the side, or crumble some over top before serving.

Cooking oil	1 tsp.	5 mL
Lean ground beef	3/4 lb.	340 g
Can of pinto beans, rinsed and drained	14 oz.	398 mL
Taco seasoning mix, stir before measuring	2 tbsp.	30 mL
Ranch dressing	1/4 cup	60 mL
Lime juice	2 tbsp.	30 mL
Sour cream	2 tbsp.	30 mL
Taco seasoning mix, stir before measuring	1 tbsp.	15 mL
Iceberg lettuce mix	8 cups	2 L
Chopped tomato	2 cups	500 mL
Diced green pepper	2 cups	500 mL
Diced avocado	1 1/3 cups	325 mL
Grated Monterey Jack cheese	1 cup	250 mL

Heat cooking oil in large frying pan on medium-high. Add beef. Scramble-fry for about 8 minutes until no longer pink.

Add beans and first amount of taco seasoning. Stir.

Combine next 4 ingredients in extra-large bowl.

Add remaining 5 ingredients and beef mixture. Toss. Serve immediately. Makes about 10 cups (2.5 L).

1 1/2 cups (375 mL): 351 Calories; 21.1 g Total Fat (3.4 g Mono, 1.4 g Poly, 7.1 g Sat); 53 mg Cholesterol; 22 g Carbohydrate; 8 g Fibre; 19 g Protein; 573 mg Sodium

Wild Mushroom Arugula Salad

This green salad features earthy mushrooms and sirloin strips. The bright flavours of balsamic and lemon add unexpected freshness, while Brie provides a creamy complement.

Arugula, lightly packed	8 cups	2 L
Seasoned croutons	2 cups	500 mL
Sliced fresh oyster mushrooms	1 cup	250 mL
Sliced fresh shiitake mushrooms	1 cup	250 mL
Brie cheese round, chopped	4 oz.	125 g
Cooking oil	2 tbsp.	30 mL
Beef top sirloin steak, cut into thin, short strips	3/4 lb.	340 g
Salt	1/2 tsp.	2 mL
Pepper	1/8 tsp.	0.5 mL
Finely chopped onion	2 tbsp.	30 mL
Garlic clove, minced (or 1/4 tsp., 1 mL, powder)	1	1
Balsamic vinegar	1/3 cup	75 mL
Chopped fresh thyme	1 tbsp.	15 mL
Lemon juice	2 tsp.	10 mL

Toss first 5 ingredients in extra-large bowl.

Heat large frying pan or wok on medium-high until very hot. Add cooking oil. Add beef. Sprinkle with salt and pepper. Stir-fry for 2 minutes. Transfer with slotted spoon to plate. Reduce heat to medium.

Add onion and garlic to same frying pan. Cook for about 1 minute, stirring often, until onion is softened. Add vinegar. Heat and stir, scraping any brown bits from bottom of pan, until boiling. Remove from heat.

Add thyme, lemon juice and beef. Stir. Add to arugula mixture. Toss gently. Serve immediately. Makes about 10 cups (2.5 L).

1 1/2 cups (375 mL): 252 Calories; 14.9 g Total Fat (6.4 g Mono, 1.8 g Poly, 5.3 g Sat); 45 mg Cholesterol; 12 g Carbohydrate; 2 g Fibre; 17 g Protein; 465 mg Sodium

Pictured on page 36.

Denver Salad

An intriguing take on a breakfast classic. This Denver omelette-inspired brunch salad is an easy combination of simple, flavourful ingredients, such as crunchy lettuce and peppers, egg ribbons and smoky ham.

Romaine and iceberg lettuce mix, lightly packed	6 cups	1.5 L
Diced cooked ham	2 cups	500 mL
Diced green pepper	1 cup	250 mL
Diced red pepper	1 cup	250 mL
Sliced green onion	1/2 cup	125 mL
Large eggs	4	4
Water	1 tbsp.	15 mL
Salt, sprinkle		
Pepper, sprinkle		
Butter (or hard margarine)	1 tbsp.	15 mL
Italian dressing	1/3 cup	75 mL

Toss first 5 ingredients in extra-large bowl.

Whisk next 4 ingredients in small bowl.

Melt butter in large non-stick frying pan on medium. Pour egg mixture into pan. Reduce heat to medium-low. When starting to set at outside edge, tilt pan and gently lift cooked egg mixture with spatula, easing around pan from outside edge in. Allow uncooked egg mixture to flow onto bottom of pan, until egg is softly set. Cook, covered, for about 1 minute until top is set. Transfer to cutting board. Let stand until cool. Slice into thin ribbons.

Add dressing to lettuce mixture. Toss. Scatter egg ribbons over top. Makes about 10 1/2 cups (2.6 L).

1 1/2 cups (375 mL): 205 Calories; 14.2 g Total Fat (3.5 g Mono, 0.8 g Poly, 4.8 g Sat); 163 mg Cholesterol; 5 g Carbohydrate; 2 g Fibre; 15 g Protein; 210 mg Sodium

Paré Pointer

There are twenty million eggs in New Yolk City.

"Stir-Fry" Beef Salad

This Asian-style salad is so easy to toss together for a fun and tasty potluck option—all your favourite stir-fry flavours in a crisp, cold salad.

Chopped or torn iceberg lettuce, lightly packed	8 cups	2 L
Julienned cooked roast beef	1 1/2 cups	375 mL
Fresh bean sprouts	1 cup	250 mL
Snow peas, trimmed and halved	1 cup	250 mL
Thinly sliced red pepper	1 cup	250 mL
Julienned carrot	1/2 cup	125 mL
Thinly sliced red onion	1/2 cup	125 mL
Asian-style sesame dressing	1/2 cup	125 mL

Toss first 7 ingredients in extra-large bowl.

Add dressing. Toss. Makes about 16 cups (4 L).

1 1/2 cups (375 mL): 111 Calories; 5.3 g Total Fat (1.1 g Mono, 0.2 g Poly, 1.4 g Sat); 16 mg Cholesterol; 8 g Carbohydrate; 1 g Fibre; 9 g Protein; 154 mg Sodium

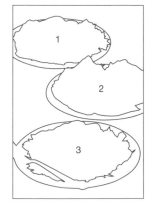

1. Blue Cheese Tenderloin Salad, page 23
2. Turkey Ribbon Salad, page 29
3. Strawberry Pork Salad, page 22

Props: TAG

Spanakopita Salad

A take on the tasty spinach pie (span-uh-KOH-pih-tuh), without the fussy phyllo! This fresh spinach and feta blend is surrounded by pita crisps for the perfect lunch salad.

Pita breads (7 inch, 18 cm, diameter), split	2	2
Butter (or hard margarine), melted	1 tbsp.	15 mL
Greek seasoning	1 tsp.	5 mL
Baby spinach leaves, lightly packed	8 cups	2 L
Diced feta cheese	1 cup	250 mL
Balsamic vinaigrette dressing	1/2 cup	125 mL
Thinly sliced red onion	1/4 cup	60 mL
Chopped fresh mint	3 tbsp.	50 mL
Pine nuts, toasted (see Tip, page 134)	2 tbsp.	30 mL

Brush one side of each pita with butter. Sprinkle with Greek seasoning. Arrange on ungreased baking sheet. Bake in 400°F (205°C) oven for about 3 minutes until golden. Let stand for about 10 minutes until crisp. Break into large pieces.

Toss next 5 ingredients in large bowl. Transfer to 4 serving plates. Arrange pita pieces around edge of each plate.

Sprinkle with pine nuts. Serves 4.

1 serving: 349 Calories; 22.1 g Total Fat (3.3 g Mono, 2.0 g Poly, 8.7 g Sat); 41 mg Cholesterol; 29 g Carbohydrate; 3 g Fibre; 10 g Protein; 977 mg Sodium

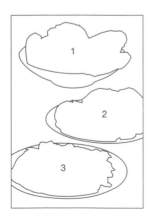

1. African Chickpea Salad, page 113
2. Melon Shrimp Salad, page 42
3. Mustard Halibut Salad, page 33

Props: Sango
      Mikasa

BLT Salad

Who doesn't love a fresh and toasty BLT? This fabulous salad has everything that makes BLTs so delectable—chewy bacon, crisp lettuce and cherry tomatoes with French bread croutons.

SEASONED CROUTONS

Butter (or hard margarine), softened	1/4 cup	60 mL
Grated Parmesan cheese	3 tbsp.	50 mL
Italian seasoning	1 1/2 tsp.	7 mL
Worcestershire sauce	1 tsp.	5 mL
French bread slices (about 1 inch, 2.5 cm, thick)	5	5

SALAD

Bacon slices, cut into 2 inch (5 cm) pieces	12	12
Cut or torn romaine (or iceberg) lettuce, lightly packed	8 cups	2 L
Cherry tomatoes, halved	3 cups	750 mL
Fresh spinach leaves, lightly packed	2 cups	500 mL

TANGY MAYO DRESSING

Buttermilk	1/3 cup	75 mL
Mayonnaise	1/4 cup	60 mL
Apple cider vinegar	2 tbsp.	30 mL
Garlic powder	1/2 tsp	2 mL
Granulated sugar	1/2 tsp.	2 mL
Pepper	1/8 tsp.	0.5 mL

Seasoned Croutons: Combine first 4 ingredients in small bowl. Spread over both sides of bread slices. Cut into 1 inch (2.5 cm) pieces. Arrange on greased baking sheet with sides. Bake in 300°F (150°C) oven for about 25 minutes, stirring occasionally, until toasted. Let stand until cool. Makes about 4 cups (1 L).

Salad: Cook bacon in large frying pan on medium until crisp. Transfer with slotted spoon to paper towel-lined plate to drain. Transfer to extra-large bowl.

Add remaining 3 ingredients. Toss.

(continued on next page)

Leafy Greens

Tangy Mayo Dressing: Whisk all 6 ingredients in small bowl. Makes about 2/3 cup (150 mL). Add with Seasoned Croutons to salad. Toss gently. Makes about 14 cups (3.5 L).

1 1/2 cups (375 mL): 260 Calories; 15.2 g Total Fat (3.3 g Mono, 1.0 g Poly, 5.7 g Sat); 27 mg Cholesterol; 23 g Carbohydrate; 3 g Fibre; 9 g Protein; 532 mg Sodium

---

Lamb Raita Salad Wraps

Curry and rich lamb are mellowed by yogurt and cucumber in these wraps inspired by raita, a cooling yogurt salad found in Indian cuisine. You could tear up the lettuce and toss it with the lamb mixture instead if you prefer.

Cooking oil	2 tsp.	10 mL
Lean ground lamb	1 lb.	454 g
Water	2 tbsp.	30 mL
Madras curry paste	1 tbsp.	15 mL
Plain yogurt	1/2 cup	125 mL
Diced English cucumber (with peel)	1/4 cup	60 mL
Diced tomato	1/4 cup	60 mL
Chopped fresh mint	1 tbsp.	15 mL
(or 3/4 tsp., 4 mL, dried)		
Chopped green onion	1 tbsp.	15 mL
Chopped unsalted, roasted cashews	1 tbsp.	15 mL
Lemon juice	2 tsp.	10 mL
Granulated sugar	1 tsp.	5 mL
Salt	1/2 tsp.	2 mL
Large green leaf lettuce leaves	8	8

Heat cooking oil in large frying pan on medium-high. Add lamb. Scramble-fry for about 8 minutes until no longer pink.

Add water and curry paste. Heat and stir for about 2 minutes until water has evaporated. Transfer to medium bowl. Cool.

Add next 9 ingredients. Stir.

Serve lamb mixture with lettuce leaves for wrapping. Makes 8 salad wraps.

1 salad wrap: 165 Calories; 11.2 g Total Fat (4.7 g Mono, 1.1 g Poly, 4.2 g Sat); 45 mg Cholesterol; 3 g Carbohydrate; trace Fibre; 12 g Protein; 282 mg Sodium

Strawberry Pork Salad

Grilled pork is at its best when tossed with fresh greens and sweet strawberries. Walnuts and goat cheese add richness and round out the flavours of this delicious, eye-catching salad.

Pork tenderloin, trimmed of fat	3/4 lb.	340 g
Salt	1/4 tsp.	1 mL
Pepper	1/8 tsp.	0.5 mL
Olive (or cooking) oil	3 tbsp.	50 mL
Strawberry jam, warmed	3 tbsp.	50 mL
White balsamic (or white wine) vinegar	2 tbsp.	30 mL
Coarsely ground pepper	1/4 tsp.	1 mL
Spring mix lettuce, lightly packed	8 cups	2 L
Sliced fresh strawberries	2/3 cup	150 mL
Walnut pieces, toasted (see Tip, page 134)	1/2 cup	125 mL
Thinly sliced celery	1/3 cup	75 mL
Thinly sliced sweet onion	1/3 cup	75 mL
Goat (chèvre) cheese, cut up	3 oz.	85 g

Preheat gas barbecue to medium (see Note). Sprinkle tenderloin with salt and pepper. Cook on greased grill for about 20 minutes, turning once, until internal temperature reaches 155°F (68°C). Transfer to cutting board. Cover with foil. Let stand for 20 minutes. Internal temperature should rise to at least 160°F (71°C). Slice thinly.

Whisk next 4 ingredients in small bowl.

Toss remaining 6 ingredients and pork in extra-large bowl. Drizzle with olive oil mixture. Toss. Makes about 10 cups (2.5 L).

1 1/2 cups (375 mL): 249 Calories; 16.7 g Total Fat (6.7 g Mono, 5.4 g Poly, 3.9 g Sat); 39 mg Cholesterol; 11 g Carbohydrate; 2 g Fibre; 15 g Protein; 172 mg Sodium

Pictured on page 17.

Note: Too cold to barbecue? Use the oven instead! Cook tenderloin in 475°F (240°C) oven for 25 to 30 minutes until internal temperature reaches 155°F (68°C). Transfer to cutting board. Cover with foil. Let stand for 20 minutes. Internal temperature should rise to at least 160°F (71°C).

Blue Cheese Tenderloin Salad

Impress your guests with this show-stopping salad—spring mix with raspberry vinaigrette alongside tenderloin medallions and cheese-topped baguette. Perfect for summer entertaining when fresh raspberries are at their peak.

Garlic powder	1/4 tsp.	1 mL
Salt	1/4 tsp.	1 mL
Pepper	1/2 tsp.	2 mL
Pork tenderloin, trimmed of fat, cut into 20 slices	3/4 lb.	340 g
Cooking oil	1 tbsp.	15 mL
Baguette bread slices (about 1/4 inch, 6 mm, thick)	20	20
Cooking oil	1 tbsp.	15 mL
Blue cheese, crumbled	4 oz.	113 g
Spring mix lettuce, lightly packed	8 cups	2 L
Raspberry vinaigrette dressing	1/3 cup	75 mL
Fresh raspberries	1 cup	250 mL

Combine first 3 ingredients in small cup. Sprinkle over pork. Heat first amount of cooking oil in large frying pan on medium-high. Add pork. Cook for about 2 minutes per side until no longer pink inside. Transfer to large plate. Let stand, uncovered, for 5 minutes.

Arrange bread slices on baking sheet with sides. Brush tops with second amount of cooking oil. Broil on centre rack in oven for about 3 minutes until golden. Remove from oven. Turn bread slices over. Sprinkle cheese over top. Broil on centre rack in oven for about 1 minute until cheese is melted.

Toss lettuce and dressing in large bowl. Transfer to 4 serving plates. Arrange bread slices, alternately with pork slices, around lettuce mixture.

Scatter raspberries over top. Serves 4.

1 serving: 497 Calories; 25.1 g Total Fat (7.5 g Mono, 2.6 g Poly, 6.8 g Sat); 82 mg Cholesterol; 41 g Carbohydrate; 2 g Fibre; 31 g Protein; 1089 mg Sodium

Pictured on page 17.

Spinach Goat Cheese Salad

An appetizing combination for the adventuresome palate. Almond-coated goat cheese and tomato chutney are served atop spinach with toasted baguette slices—a lovely presentation for a special-occasion lunch.

Olive (or cooking) oil	2 tsp.	10 mL
Finely chopped onion	1/4 cup	60 mL
Garlic clove, minced	1	1
(or 1/4 tsp., 1 mL, powder)		
Diced tomato	1 cup	250 mL
Balsamic vinegar	2 tsp.	10 mL
Brown sugar, packed	1 tsp.	5 mL
Salt	1/4 tsp.	1 mL
Pepper	1/4 tsp.	1 mL
Cayenne pepper, sprinkle		
Chopped fresh basil	2 tsp.	10 mL
(or 1/2 tsp., 2 mL, dried)		
Goat (chèvre) cheese, softened	8 oz.	225 g
Sliced natural almonds	1/2 cup	125 mL
Olive (or cooking) oil	2 tbsp.	30 mL
Lemon juice	1 tbsp.	15 mL
Salt, sprinkle		
Fresh spinach leaves, lightly packed	4 cups	1 L
Baguette bread slices, toasted	8	8

Heat first amount of olive oil in medium frying pan on medium. Add onion and garlic. Cook for about 3 minutes, stirring often, until softened.

Add next 6 ingredients. Heat and stir for 2 minutes. Cool.

Add basil. Stir.

Divide cheese into 4 equal portions. Roll each portion into ball.

Place almonds in shallow dish. Roll cheese balls in almonds until coated. Arrange on greased baking sheet with sides. Bake in 400°F (205°C) oven for about 10 minutes until almonds are lightly browned and cheese is warm.

(continued on next page)

Leafy Greens

Whisk next 3 ingredients in large bowl. Add spinach. Toss. Transfer to 4 serving plates. Spoon tomato mixture over spinach. Top with cheese balls.

Place bread slices on edge of plates. Serves 4.

1 serving: 390 Calories; 26.8 g Total Fat (12.3 g Mono, 2.8 g Poly, 10.0 g Sat); 29 mg Cholesterol; 24 g Carbohydrate; 3 g Fibre; 17 g Protein; 554 mg Sodium

Corn-on-the-Cobb Salad

Baby corn is a fun addition to this updated Cobb salad, chock full of veggies and chopped eggs. Serve with garlic toast or your favourite fresh-baked bread.

Cut or torn green leaf lettuce, lightly packed	5 cups	1.25 L
Watercress, stems removed, chopped	1/4 cup	60 mL
Sliced green onion	2 tbsp.	30 mL
Chopped cooked chicken (see Tip, page 41)	1 cup	250 mL
Diced avocado	1 cup	250 mL
Sliced celery	3/4 cup	175 mL
Canned cut baby corn, drained	1/2 cup	125 mL
Diced English cucumber (with peel)	1/2 cup	125 mL
Grated carrot	1/2 cup	125 mL
Large hard-cooked eggs, finely chopped	2	2
Blue cheese (or ranch) dressing	1/4 cup	60 mL

Toss first 3 ingredients in large bowl. Arrange on 4 serving plates.

Scatter next 7 ingredients over top.

Drizzle with dressing. Serves 4.

1 serving: 273 Calories; 18.9 g Total Fat (6.6 g Mono, 5.7 Poly, 3.8 g Sat); 141 mg Cholesterol; 12 g Carbohydrate; 4 g Fibre; 16 g Protein; 270 mg Sodium

Paré Pointer
Little Johnny wasn't pulling the cat's tail—he was just holding it. The cat was doing the pulling.

Crispy Chicken Salad

The favourite flavours of breaded chicken fingers and plum sauce are reinvented in this creatively tasty salad! Crispy chicken pieces are tossed with spring lettuce mix, veggies and zingy Asian plum dressing.

Large egg	1	1
Fine dry bread crumbs	1/2 cup	125 mL
Seasoned salt	3/4 tsp.	4 mL
Boneless, skinless chicken breast halves (4 – 6 oz., 113 – 170 g, each), cut lengthwise into 4 strips each	2	2
Cooking spray		
Apple cider vinegar	1/4 cup	60 mL
Plum jam	2 tbsp.	30 mL
Soy sauce	1 tbsp.	15 mL
Sesame oil (for flavour)	2 tsp.	10 mL
Ground ginger	1 tsp.	5 mL
Pepper	1/4 tsp.	1 mL
Spring mix lettuce, lightly packed	6 cups	1.5 L
Sugar snap peas, trimmed and halved	1/2 cup	125 mL
Thinly sliced red pepper	1/2 cup	125 mL
Thinly sliced red onion	1/4 cup	60 mL

Beat egg with fork in small bowl.

Combine bread crumbs and seasoned salt in medium shallow dish.

Dip chicken into egg. Press into bread crumb mixture until coated. Discard any remaining egg and crumb mixture. Arrange chicken on greased baking sheet with sides. Spray with cooking spray. Bake in 425°F (220°C) oven for about 15 minutes until no longer pink inside. Transfer to cutting board. Cool. Cut into 1 inch (2.5 cm) pieces.

Whisk next 6 ingredients in large bowl until smooth.

Add remaining 4 ingredients and chicken. Toss. Serve immediately. Makes about 7 cups (1.75 L).

1 cup (250 mL): 110 Calories; 2.7 g Total Fat (0.1 g Mono, 0.1 g Poly, 0.5 g Sat); 42 mg Cholesterol; 11 g Carbohydrate; 1 g Fibre; 10 g Protein; 343 mg Sodium

Summer Spinach Salad

This fresh, colourful blend includes sweet summer berries, sharp Asiago, vibrant pistachios and beautifully grilled chicken—truly a light and easy meal salad to enjoy on the patio.

Boneless, skinless chicken breast halves	1 lb.	454 g
Salt	1/4 tsp.	1 mL
Pepper	1/4 tsp.	1 mL
Fresh spinach leaves, lightly packed	6 cups	1.5 L
Fresh blueberries	1/2 cup	125 mL
Fresh raspberries	1/2 cup	125 mL
Thinly sliced red onion	1/2 cup	125 mL
Grated Asiago cheese	1/4 cup	60 mL
Pistachios	1/4 cup	60 mL
Lemon juice	3 tbsp.	50 mL
Olive (or cooking) oil	3 tbsp.	50 mL
Dijon mustard	2 tsp.	10 mL
Liquid honey	2 tsp.	10 mL
Grated lemon zest	1 tsp.	5 mL
Garlic clove, minced	1	1
(or 1/4 tsp., 1 mL, powder)		
Salt	1/4 tsp.	1 mL

Sprinkle both sides of chicken with salt and pepper. Preheat gas barbecue to medium (see Tip, page 50). Cook chicken on greased grill for about 7 minutes per side until internal temperature reaches 170°F (77°C). Transfer to cutting board. Cool. Cut into 1/2 inch (12 mm) slices. Transfer to large bowl.

Add next 6 ingredients.

Whisk remaining 7 ingredients in small bowl. Drizzle over spinach mixture. Toss gently. Makes about 9 cups (2.25 L).

1 cup (250 mL): 151 Calories; 8.0 g Total Fat (4.4 g Mono, 1.4 g Poly, 1.6 g Sat); 32 mg Cholesterol; 7 g Carbohydrate; 1 g Fibre; 14 g Protein; 223 mg Sodium

Pictured on page 90.

Chicken Pecan Salad

The highlight of this light and fresh green salad is the smooth-tasting Dijon dressing which coats toasty pecans and bites of tender chicken.

Cut or torn romaine lettuce, lightly packed	8 cups	2 L
Chopped cooked chicken (see Tip, page 41)	1 cup	250 mL
Pecan halves, toasted (see Tip, page 134)	1 cup	250 mL
Thinly sliced English cucumber (with peel)	1/2 cup	125 mL
Thinly sliced red onion	1/4 cup	60 mL
Medium tomatoes, cut into 8 wedges each	2	2
MUSTARD DRESSING		
Cooking oil	1/4 cup	60 mL
Dijon mustard (with whole seeds)	2 tbsp.	30 mL
White wine vinegar	1 1/2 tbsp.	25 mL
Granulated sugar	1/2 tsp.	2 mL
Dried basil	1/8 tsp.	0.5 mL
Small garlic clove, minced (or 1/8 tsp., 0.5 mL, powder)	1	1
Salt	1/8 tsp.	0.5 mL
Pepper, sprinkle		

Toss first 6 ingredients in extra-large bowl.

Mustard Dressing: Whisk all 8 ingredients in small bowl. Makes about 1/2 cup (125 mL). Drizzle over lettuce mixture. Toss. Makes about 10 cups (2.5 L).

1 1/2 cups (375 mL): 253 Calories; 22.6 g Total Fat (12.2 g Mono, 6.5 g Poly, 2.3 g Sat); 20 mg Cholesterol; 8 g Carbohydrate; 3 g Fibre; 8 g Protein; 127 mg Sodium

Paré Pointer

His classroom is like an old car—full of nuts with a crank in the front.

Leafy Greens

Turkey Ribbon Salad

A colourful, inviting salad with marinated turkey, cucumber strips and tangy dressing over a butter lettuce bed. Use a vegetable peeler on a piece of Parmesan to create the lovely shaved pieces.

Olive (or cooking) oil	1/2 cup	125 mL
Red wine vinegar	1/4 cup	60 mL
Grated onion	2 tbsp.	30 mL
Dijon mustard	1 tbsp.	15 mL
Granulated sugar	1 tsp.	5 mL
Salt	1/2 tsp.	2 mL
Pepper	1/4 tsp.	1 mL
Turkey scaloppine	3/4 lb.	340 g
Small English cucumber (with peel)	1/2	1/2
Grated carrot	1/2 cup	125 mL
Butter lettuce leaves	20	20
Shaved Parmesan cheese	1/2 cup	125 mL

Whisk first 7 ingredients in small bowl.

Place turkey in large shallow bowl. Pour 1/2 cup (125 mL) olive oil mixture over top. Turn until coated. Marinate, covered, in refrigerator for 30 minutes. Transfer turkey to greased wire rack set on baking sheet with sides. Discard any remaining marinade. Broil turkey on top rack in oven for about 3 minutes until no longer pink inside. Transfer to cutting board. Let stand until cool enough to handle. Cut into 1/2 inch (12 mm) strips. Transfer to medium bowl.

Peel cucumber into long strips with vegetable peeler. Add to turkey. Add carrot and remaining olive oil mixture. Toss.

Arrange 5 lettuce leaves on each of 4 serving plates. Top with turkey mixture. Scatter cheese over top. Serves 4.

1 serving: 380 Calories; 30.8 g Total Fat (18.0 g Mono, 3.7 g Poly, 6.6 g Sat); 53 mg Cholesterol; 8 g Carbohydrate; 1 g Fibre; 24 g Protein; 1495 mg Sodium

Pictured on page 17.

Parisian Luncheon Salad

Tangy herb vinaigrette dresses up a pretty, layered tuna salad.

Cooking oil	1 tsp.	5 mL
Large eggs, fork-beaten	2	2
Pepper	1/8 tsp.	0.5 mL
Butter lettuce leaves	24	24
Grated carrot	1 cup	250 mL
Can of solid white tuna in water, drained, broken into chunks	6 oz.	170 g
Thinly sliced red onion, separated into rings	1/3 cup	75 mL
Cherry tomatoes, halved	6	6
TANGY TARRAGON VINAIGRETTE		
Olive (or cooking) oil	4 tsp.	20 mL
Balsamic vinegar	1 tbsp.	15 mL
Chopped fresh parsley (or 3/4 tsp., 4 mL, dried)	1 tbsp.	15 mL
Lemon juice	1 tbsp.	15 mL
White wine vinegar	1 tbsp.	15 mL
Chopped fresh tarragon (or 1/4 tsp., 1 mL, dried)	1 tsp.	5 mL
Garlic clove, minced (or 1/4 tsp., 1 mL, powder)	1	1
Salt	1/4 tsp.	1 mL

Heat cooking oil in small non-stick frying pan on medium. Add egg. Sprinkle with pepper. Reduce heat to medium-low. When starting to set at outside edge, tilt pan and gently lift cooked egg with spatula, easing around pan from outside edge in. Allow uncooked egg to flow onto bottom of pan until egg is softly set. Cook, covered, for about 1 minute until top is set. Transfer to cutting board. Let stand until cool. Slice into thin ribbons.

Arrange lettuce on 4 serving plates. Scatter next 4 ingredients over lettuce. Top with egg ribbons.

Tangy Tarragon Vinaigrette: Whisk all 8 ingredients in small bowl. Makes about 1/3 cup (75 mL). Drizzle over egg ribbons. Serves 4.

1 serving: 171 Calories; 9.6 g Total Fat (4.4 g Mono, 1.6 g Poly, 1.9 g Sat); 125 mg Cholesterol; 7 g Carbohydrate; 2 g Fibre; 14 g Protein; 363 mg Sodium

Summer Shrimp Salad

Subtle, sweet dressing highlights the fresh flavours of shrimp, cherry tomatoes and vibrant butter lettuce in this light meal salad.

Olive (or cooking) oil	3 tbsp.	50 mL
Lemon juice	1 tbsp.	15 mL
White wine vinegar	1 tbsp.	15 mL
Dijon mustard	2 tsp.	10 mL
Granulated sugar	1 tsp.	5 mL
Garlic clove, minced	1	1
(or 1/4 tsp., 1 mL, powder)		
Salt	1/2 tsp.	2 mL
Pepper	1/4 tsp.	1 mL
Cut or torn butter lettuce, lightly packed	8 cups	2 L
Cooked medium shrimp	3/4 lb.	340 g
(peeled and deveined)		
Quartered cherry tomatoes	1 cup	250 mL
Sliced English cucumber (with peel),	1/2 cup	125 mL
halved lengthwise before slicing		
Thinly sliced green onion	2 tbsp.	30 mL

Whisk first 8 ingredients in extra-large bowl.

Add remaining 5 ingredients. Toss gently. Serve immediately. Makes about 12 cups (3 L).

1 1/2 cups (375 mL): 105 Calories; 6.2 g Total Fat (3.9 g Mono, 1.1 g Poly, 0.9 g Sat); 65 mg Cholesterol; 3 g Carbohydrate; 1 g Fibre; 10 g Protein; 228 mg Sodium

Paré Pointer
If you really want to rock and roll, put wheels on a rocking chair.

Fish and Chips Salad

An all-time pub favourite with a twist! Firm haddock is breaded in crispy potato chips, and served atop fresh greens and peas with a tartar sauce dressing.

All-purpose flour	1/4 cup	60 mL
Lemon pepper	1/2 tsp.	2 mL
Large egg	1	1
Crushed salt and vinegar flavoured potato chips (about 4 cups, 1 L, uncrushed)	1 1/2 cups	375 mL
Haddock fillets, any small bones removed, cut into 1 1/2 inch (3.8 cm) pieces	3/4 lb.	340 g
Olive (or cooking) oil	1 tbsp.	15 mL
Cut or torn romaine lettuce, lightly packed	6 cups	1.5 L
Diced yellow pepper	1/2 cup	125 mL
Frozen tiny peas, thawed	1/2 cup	125 mL
Olive (or cooking) oil	3 tbsp.	50 mL
Lemon juice	2 tbsp.	30 mL
Tartar sauce	2 tbsp.	30 mL
Finely diced onion	1 tbsp.	15 mL
White vinegar	1 tbsp.	15 mL
Granulated sugar	1 tsp.	5 mL
Salt	1/4 tsp.	1 mL
Pepper	1/4 tsp.	1 mL

Combine flour and lemon pepper in small shallow dish.

Beat egg with fork in small bowl.

Place potato chips in medium shallow dish.

Press fish into flour until coated. Dip into egg. Press fish into chips until coated. Discard any remaining flour mixture, egg and potato chips.

Heat first amount of olive oil in large frying pan on medium. Add fish. Cook for 3 minutes per side until golden and fish flakes easily when tested with fork.

Toss next 3 ingredients in large bowl.

(continued on next page)

Leafy Greens

Whisk remaining 8 ingredients in small bowl. Drizzle over lettuce mixture. Toss. Arrange on 4 serving plates. Top with fish. Serve immediately. Serves 4.

1 serving: 486 Calories; 32 g Total Fat (12.8 g Mono, 9.8 g Poly, 6.2 g Sat); 91 mg Cholesterol; 31 g Carbohydrate; 5 g Fibre; 23 g Protein; 724 mg Sodium

Mustard Halibut Salad

Honey mustard-marinated fish with a light crunch of toasted almonds is paired with crisp vegetables and a sprinkle of Asiago. This vibrantly colourful salad offers a wonderful combination of flavours and textures.

Dijon mustard (with whole seeds)	1/4 cup	60 mL
Liquid honey	2 tbsp.	30 mL
Salt	1/4 tsp.	1 mL
Pepper	1/4 tsp.	1 mL
Sliced almonds, crushed	1 1/4 cups	300 mL
Halibut fillets, any small bones removed, cut into 1 inch (2.5 cm) pieces, blotted dry	3/4 lb.	340 g
Olive (or cooking) oil	3 tbsp.	50 mL
Lemon juice	2 tbsp.	30 mL
Romaine lettuce mix, lightly packed	6 cups	1.5 L
Thinly sliced red pepper	2 cups	500 mL
Grated Asiago cheese	1/2 cup	125 mL

Combine first 4 ingredients in medium bowl. Reserve 1 tbsp. (15 mL).

Place almonds in medium shallow dish.

Add fish to remaining mustard mixture. Toss until coated. Press fish into almonds until coated. Discard remaining mustard mixture and almonds. Arrange fish on greased baking sheet with sides. Bake in 450°F (230°C) oven for about 7 minutes until fish flakes easily when tested with fork.

Whisk olive oil, lemon juice and reserved mustard mixture in large bowl. Add remaining 3 ingredients. Toss. Arrange on 4 serving plates. Top with fish. Serves 4.

1 serving: 452 Calories; 30.8 g Total Fat (16.2 g Mono, 5.5 g Poly, 5.3 g Sat); 40 mg Cholesterol; 20 g Carbohydrate; 7 g Fibre; 28 g Protein; 446 mg Sodium

Pictured on page 18.

My Monday Mimosa

This lovely salad, its delicate egg yolk garnish named for the yellow mimosa flower, is ideal for packing up on Monday morning to take for lunch. Store the lettuce mixture, dressing and egg yolk in separate containers and combine just before eating.

Cut or torn butter lettuce, lightly packed	1 cup	250 mL
Arugula, lightly packed	1/2 cup	125 mL
Chopped cooked salad shrimp	1/2 cup	125 mL
Ranch dressing	2 tbsp.	30 mL
Hard-cooked egg yolk (large), see Note	1	1

Toss first 3 ingredients in medium bowl.

Add dressing. Toss gently. Transfer to serving plate.

Press egg yolk through sieve over lettuce mixture. Serves 1.

1 serving: 358 Calories; 29.3 g Total Fat (4.2 g Mono, 5.0 g Poly, 5.3 g Sat); 324 mg Cholesterol; 6 g Carbohydrate; 1 g Fibre; 18 g Protein; 495 mg Sodium

Note: The hard-cooked egg white can also be included for an added protein boost.

1. Pesto Veggie Steak Salad, page 136
2. Chicken Fajita Salad, page 78

Props: bianco nero

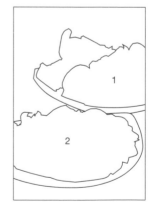

Buttermilk Spinach Salad

A traditional spinach and egg salad makes for a protein-packed meal—the creamy buttermilk dressing has a pleasing garlic flavour.

Fresh spinach leaves, lightly packed	10 cups	2.5 L
Thinly sliced fresh white mushrooms	1 1/2 cups	375 mL
Grated medium Cheddar cheese	3/4 cup	175 mL
Thinly sliced red onion	1/2 cup	125 mL
Large hard-cooked eggs, chopped	4	4
BUTTERMILK DRESSING		
Buttermilk	2/3 cup	150 mL
Mayonnaise	2 tbsp.	30 mL
Dijon mustard	1 tsp.	5 mL
White wine vinegar	1 tsp.	5 mL
Garlic clove, minced	1	1
(or 1/4 tsp., 1 mL, powder)		
Salt	1/4 tsp.	1 mL
Pepper	1/4 tsp.	1 mL

Toss first 5 ingredients in extra-large bowl.

Buttermilk Dressing: Whisk all 7 ingredients in small bowl until smooth. Makes about 3/4 cup (175 mL). Add to spinach mixture. Toss. Makes about 12 cups (3 L).

1 1/2 cups (375 mL): *133 Calories; 9.5 g Total Fat (2.1 g Mono, 0.5 g Poly, 3.7 g Sat); 120 mg Cholesterol; 4 g Carbohydrate; 1 g Fibre; 8 g Protein; 245 mg Sodium*

Variation: Add 1/2 cup (125 mL) toasted sunflower seeds (see Tip, page 134).

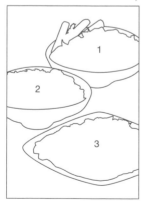

1. Wild Mushroom Arugula Salad, page 14
2. Olé Barley Salad, page 116
3. Sunshine Salmon Salad, page 49

Props: Studio Nova

Aussie Burger Salad

Inspired by Australian burgers, often served with beets and fried egg right in the bun! Lamb and feta patties are served alongside pickled beets, shredded lettuce and herbs for a variety of complementary flavours. If you prefer to barbecue the patties, grill them on greased foil.

Large egg, fork-beaten	1	1
Fine dry bread crumbs	1/4 cup	60 mL
Chopped fresh mint	1 tbsp.	15 mL
(or 3/4 tsp., 4 mL, dried)		
Dijon mustard	1 1/2 tsp.	7 mL
Lean ground lamb (or beef)	1/2 lb.	225 g
Crumbled feta cheese	1/2 cup	125 mL
Cooking oil	1 tsp.	5 mL
Shredded romaine lettuce, lightly packed	5 cups	1.25 L
Cherry tomatoes, halved	1 cup	250 mL
Balsamic vinaigrette dressing	1/3 cup	75 mL
Thinly sliced green onion	1/4 cup	60 mL
Chopped fresh mint	1 tbsp.	15 mL
(or 3/4 tsp., 4 mL, dried)		
Chopped fresh parsley	1 tbsp.	15 mL
(or 3/4 tsp., 4 mL, dried)		
Bacon slices, cooked crisp and crumbled	4	4
Sliced pickled beets, rinsed and drained	1 cup	250 mL
Large hard-cooked eggs, quartered	4	4

Combine first 4 ingredients in medium bowl. Add lamb and cheese. Mix well. Divide into 12 equal portions. Shape into 2 inch (5 cm) patties.

Heat cooking oil in large frying pan on medium. Add patties. Cook for about 3 minutes per side until browned and internal temperature reaches 160°F (70°C). Transfer to paper towel-lined plate to drain. Cover to keep warm.

Toss next 7 ingredients in large bowl. Transfer to 4 serving plates.

Arrange beets, egg and patties over lettuce mixture. Serves 4.

1 serving: 423 Calories; 26.0 g Total Fat (4.8 g Mono, 1.6 g Poly, 8.8 g Sat); 326 mg Cholesterol; 20 g Carbohydrate; 3 g Fibre; 27 g Protein; 783 mg Sodium

Pictured on page 71.

Leafy Greens

Berry Brie Salad

A sweet-tart vinaigrette accents beautiful fruit and mild cheese, summer-fresh flavours enhanced by wonderfully aromatic raisin bread croutons. If you come across golden raspberries, try using half red and half golden.

CINNAMON RAISIN CROUTONS

Butter	1/4 cup	60 mL
Ground cinnamon	1/4 tsp.	1 mL
Raisin bread slices, cubed	4	4

SWEET RASPBERRY VINAIGRETTE

Seedless raspberry jam	2 tbsp.	30 mL
Raspberry vinegar	2 tbsp.	30 mL
Cooking oil	2 tbsp.	30 mL
Salt	1/4 tsp.	1 mL
Pepper	1/8 tsp.	0.5 mL

SALAD

Cut or torn butter lettuce, lightly packed	8 cups	2 L
Fresh raspberries	2 cups	500 mL
Fresh strawberries, sliced	2 cups	500 mL
Fresh blueberries	1 cup	250 mL
Sliced natural almonds, toasted (see Tip, page 134)	2/3 cup	150 mL
Brie cheese round, chopped	4 oz.	125 g
Chopped fresh basil, lightly packed	1/4 cup	60 mL

Cinnamon Raisin Croutons: Melt butter in large frying pan on medium. Add cinnamon. Stir. Add bread cubes. Heat and stir for about 3 minutes until golden. Transfer to paper towel-lined plate. Let stand until cool. Makes about 3 cups (750 mL).

Sweet Raspberry Vinaigrette: Whisk all 5 ingredients in small bowl. Makes about 1/3 cup (75 mL).

Salad: Toss all 7 ingredients in extra-large bowl. Add Cinnamon Raisin Croutons and Sweet Raspberry Vinaigrette. Toss. Makes about 16 cups (4 L).

1 1/2 cups (375 mL): 207 Calories; 13.9 g Total Fat (5.9 g Mono, 2.0 g Poly, 5.1 g Sat); 22 mg Cholesterol; 18 g Carbohydrate; 3 g Fibre; 6 g Protein; 230 mg Sodium

Pictured on page 107 and on back cover.

Scarlet Fruit Salad

With its delightful presentation and sophisticated flavour layers, this grown-up fruit salad is perfect for a summertime brunch.

Dried cranberries	1 cup	250 mL
Cranberry cocktail	2/3 cup	150 mL
Port wine	1/2 cup	125 mL
Balsamic vinegar	1/4 cup	60 mL
Ground cinnamon	1 tsp.	5 mL
Mini seedless watermelons	2	2
Fresh strawberries, quartered	2 cups	500 mL
Chopped Brie cheese (1/2 inch, 12 mm, pieces)	1 cup	250 mL

Combine first 5 ingredients in small saucepan. Bring to a boil. Reduce heat to medium. Boil gently, uncovered, for about 15 minutes until liquid is almost evaporated. Transfer to large bowl. Let stand until cool.

Trim thin slice from both ends of each watermelon. Cut zigzag pattern crosswise around centre of each watermelon (see diagram). Carefully split each watermelon in half. Scoop out flesh. Chop coarsely. Add 4 cups (1 L) to cranberry mixture (see Note 1). Place watermelon halves, zigzag-side up, in 4 shallow bowls (see Note 2).

Add strawberries to watermelon mixture. Stir gently. Chill for 30 minutes to blend flavours. Spoon into watermelon halves.

Scatter cheese over top. Serves 4.

1 serving: 450 Calories; 10.2 g Total Fat (2.9 g Mono, 0.4 g Poly, 6.3 g Sat); 36 mg Cholesterol; 88 g Carbohydrate; 7 g Fibre; 10 g Protein; 251 mg Sodium

Note 1: Reserve remaining watermelon for another use.

Note 2: If mini watermelons are not available, substitute 4 cups (1 L) of chopped watermelon and serve in your best bowls.

Pictured on page 53.

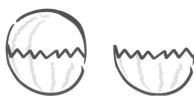

Polynesian Chicken Salad

Rich, creamy curry dressing coats tender chicken and tangy tropical fruits.
Cashews and coconut add toasted flavour and a welcome crunch.

TOASTED CURRY DRESSING

Curry powder	1 1/2 tsp.	7 mL
Mayonnaise	2/3 cup	150 mL
Milk	2 tbsp.	30 mL
Granulated sugar	4 tsp.	20 mL
Worcestershire sauce	1/2 tsp.	2 mL

SALAD

Fresh spinach leaves, lightly packed	3 cups	750 mL
Chopped cooked chicken (see Tip, below)	2 cups	500 mL
Can of pineapple tidbits, drained	14 oz.	398 mL
Can of mandarin orange segments, drained	10 oz.	284 mL
Unsalted, roasted cashews	1 cup	250 mL
Medium unsweetened coconut, toasted (see Tip, page 134)	1/2 cup	125 mL

Toasted Curry Dressing: Heat small frying pan on medium-low. Add curry powder. Heat and stir for about 5 minutes until fragrant. Transfer to small bowl. Cool.

Add remaining 4 ingredients. Stir well. Chill for 30 minutes to blend flavours. Makes about 3/4 cup (175 mL).

Salad: Toss all 6 ingredients in large bowl. Add Toasted Curry Dressing. Stir. Makes about 7 cups (1.75 L).

1 cup (250 mL): 432 Calories; 32.3 g Total Fat (6.6 g Mono, 2.3 g Poly, 8.0 g Sat); 43 mg Cholesterol; 22 g Carbohydrate; 3 g Fibre; 16 g Protein; 178 mg Sodium

 tip   Don't have any leftover chicken? Start with two boneless, skinless chicken breast halves (4 – 6 oz., 113 – 117 g, each). Place in large frying pan with 1 cup (250 mL) water or chicken broth. Simmer, covered, for 12 to 14 minutes until no longer pink inside. Drain. Chop. Makes about 2 cups (500 mL) of cooked chicken.

Melon Shrimp Salad

Cucumber and melon infuse this colourful salad with freshness. Tossed with fresh mint and crunchy peanuts, it's the perfect summertime lunch.

Cubed honeydew (3/4 inch, 2 cm, pieces)	2 cups	500 mL
Cubed watermelon (3/4 inch, 2 cm, pieces)	2 cups	500 mL
Diced English cucumber (with peel)	1 cup	250 mL
Lime juice	1/3 cup	75 mL
Cooking oil	2 tbsp.	30 mL
Finely grated ginger root	1 tsp.	5 mL
Granulated sugar	1 tsp.	5 mL
Chili paste (sambal oelek)	1/2 tsp.	2 mL
Garlic clove, minced	1	1
(or 1/4 tsp., 1 mL, powder)		
Uncooked large shrimp	1 lb.	454 g
(peeled and deveined)		
Bamboo skewers (8 inches, 20 cm, each),	8	8
soaked in water for 10 minutes		
Chopped unsalted peanuts, toasted	1/4 cup	60 mL
(see Tip, page 134)		
Finely chopped green onion	1/4 cup	60 mL
Chopped fresh mint	2 tbsp.	30 mL
Hoisin sauce	2 tbsp.	30 mL

Toss first 3 ingredients in large bowl. Let stand in refrigerator for 30 minutes. Drain.

Combine next 6 ingredients in small bowl. Transfer 2 tbsp. (30 mL) to small cup. Set aside.

Place shrimp in medium shallow dish. Pour remaining lime juice mixture over top. Stir until coated. Marinate, covered, in refrigerator for 30 minutes, stirring occasionally. Remove shrimp. Discard any remaining lime juice mixture. Thread shrimp onto skewers. Preheat gas barbecue to medium-high (see Tip, page 50). Cook shrimp on greased grill for about 2 minutes per side until shrimp turn pink. Let stand until cool enough to handle. Remove shrimp from skewers.

Add next 3 ingredients and shrimp to honeydew mixture.

(continued on next page)

Fruit

Add hoisin sauce to reserved lime juice mixture. Stir. Pour over honeydew mixture. Stir gently. Makes about 8 cups (2 L).

1 cup (250 mL): 125 Calories; 3.5 g Total Fat (1.4 g Mono, 1.2 g Poly, 0.5 g Sat); 86 mg Cholesterol; 12 g Carbohydrate; 1 g Fibre; 13 g Protein; 230 mg Sodium

Pictured on page 18.

Peppered Fruit Salad

This twist on fruit salad has a unique appearance and taste, and features the earthy contrast of pepper-coated goat cheese. Try with seasonal fruits, or anything you have on hand.

Cubed cantaloupe (3/4 inch, 2 cm, pieces)	1 cup	250 mL
Cubed fresh pineapple (3/4 inch, 2 cm, pieces)	1 cup	250 mL
Cubed honeydew (3/4 inch, 2 cm, pieces)	1 cup	250 mL
Cubed watermelon (3/4 inch, 2 cm, pieces)	1 cup	250 mL
Red seedless grapes	1 cup	250 mL
Soft goat (chèvre) cheese	4 oz.	113 g
Coarsely ground pepper	1 tbsp.	15 mL
Lime juice	1/4 cup	60 mL
Granulated sugar	2 tbsp.	30 mL
Chopped fresh mint	1 tbsp.	15 mL

Toss first 5 ingredients in large bowl. Chill for 30 minutes. Drain.

Roll cheese into balls, using 1 tsp. (5 mL) for each. Roll in pepper to coat. Chill for 30 minutes.

Whisk lime juice and sugar in small bowl until sugar is dissolved. Add to cantaloupe mixture. Stir.

Add mint and cheese balls. Toss gently. Makes about 6 cups (1.5 L).

1 cup (250 mL): 130 Calories; 4.2 g Total Fat (0.9 g Mono, 0.2 g Poly, 2.8 g Sat); 9 mg Cholesterol; 21 g Carbohydrate; 2 g Fibre; 4 g Protein; 81 mg Sodium

Pictured on page 53.

Waldorf Salad Parfaits

Inspired by the famous Waldorf salad, these parfaits are a fresh blend of crisp fruit, creamy dressing and crunchy praline walnuts. Showcase the layers in glass dishes for a special-occasion brunch.

Butter	2 tsp.	10 mL
Brown sugar, packed	1/4 cup	60 mL
Walnut halves	3/4 cup	175 mL
Lemon juice	1 tbsp.	15 mL
Granulated sugar	1/2 tsp.	2 mL
Diced fresh unpeeled pear	2 cups	500 mL
Diced unpeeled cooking apple (such as McIntosh)	2 cups	500 mL
Dried cranberries	1/4 cup	60 mL
Plain yogurt	1/4 cup	60 mL
Mayonnaise	2 tbsp.	30 mL
Shredded iceberg lettuce, lightly packed	2 cups	500 mL
Diced celery	1/2 cup	125 mL

Stir butter and brown sugar in small frying pan on medium until sugar is dissolved. Add walnuts. Stir until coated. Spread in greased foil-lined pie plate. Bake in 375°F (190°C) oven for about 8 minutes, stirring at halftime, until browned. Transfer to cutting board. Let stand until cool. Chop coarsely. Spoon half of mixture into 4 large glasses or small glass bowls.

Stir lemon juice and granulated sugar in large bowl until sugar is dissolved. Add pear and apple. Toss until coated. Add next 3 ingredients. Stir.

Layer lettuce and celery over walnut mixture. Spoon pear mixture over top. Sprinkle with remaining walnut mixture. Makes 4 salad parfaits.

1 salad parfait: 387 Calories; 22.5 g Total Fat (2.5 g Mono, 10.8 g Poly, 3.5 g Sat); 9 mg Cholesterol; 47 g Carbohydrate; 7 g Fibre; 5 g Protein; 84 mg Sodium

---

Paré Pointer

Grandpa has a wooden leg and Grandma has a cedar chest.

Strawberry Ricotta Salad Crepes

Filled with cinnamon-spiced ricotta, sweet fruit and toasted hazelnuts, these tasty bundles can be enjoyed for breakfast or brunch. This recipe is easily doubled, and the crepes and filling keep well in the fridge.

Large egg	1	1
Milk	1/2 cup	125 mL
All-purpose flour	1/4 cup	60 mL
Butter, melted	1 tbsp.	15 mL
Grated orange zest	2 tsp.	10 mL
Granulated sugar	1/2 tsp.	2 mL
Salt	1/8 tsp.	0.5 mL
Cooking oil, divided	2 tsp.	10 mL
Ricotta cheese	1/2 cup	125 mL
Flaked hazelnuts (filberts), toasted (see Tip, page 134)	2 tbsp.	30 mL
Liquid honey	1 tbsp.	15 mL
Ground cinnamon	1/4 tsp.	1 mL
Diced cantaloupe	3/4 cup	175 mL
Diced fresh strawberries	3/4 cup	175 mL

Process first 7 ingredients in blender until smooth. Chill for 30 minutes.

Heat 1/2 tsp. (2 mL) cooking oil in medium non-stick frying pan on medium. Pour about 1/4 cup (60 mL) batter into pan. Immediately tilt and swirl pan to ensure bottom is covered. Cook for about 1 minute until brown spots appear. Carefully turn crepe over. Cook for about 30 seconds until golden. Transfer to plate. Repeat with remaining batter, heating cooking oil between batches to prevent sticking.

Combine next 4 ingredients in medium bowl. Add cantaloupe and strawberries. Stir. Spoon cantaloupe mixture along centre of each crepe. Fold sides over filling. Roll up from bottom to enclose filling. Serve immediately. Makes 4 salad crepes.

1 salad crepe: 215 Calories; 12.5 g Total Fat (3.9 g Mono, 1.1 g Poly, 5.0 g Sat); 76 mg Cholesterol; 18 g Carbohydrate; 2 g Fibre; 8 g Protein; 180 mg Sodium

Avocado Orange Salad

Creamy avocado's buttery texture adds richness to tangy orange and red onion. This colourful blend also includes smoky ham and a hint of chili.

Lime juice	1/4 cup	60 mL
Liquid honey	1 tbsp.	15 mL
Chili powder	1 tsp.	5 mL
Grated orange zest	1/2 tsp.	2 mL
Dry mustard	1/4 tsp.	1 mL
Garlic clove, minced	1	1
(or 1/4 tsp., 1 mL, powder)		
Salt	1/8 tsp.	0.5 mL
Cayenne pepper, sprinkle		
Chopped avocado (3/4 inch, 2 cm, pieces)	4 cups	1 L
Black Forest ham slices, cut into thin strips	6 oz.	170 g
Sliced red onion	1/2 cup	125 mL
Medium oranges, segmented	4	4
(see Tip, page 49)		

Whisk first 8 ingredients in large bowl.

Add remaining 4 ingredients. Toss gently. Makes about 8 cups (2 L).

1 cup (250 mL): 192 Calories; 11.8 g Total Fat (7.4 g Mono, 1.4 g Poly, 2.0 g Sat); 8 mg Cholesterol; 21 g Carbohydrate; 9 g Fibre; 6 g Protein; 224 mg Sodium

Pictured on page 53.

Fruit Trio Terrine

Sweet strawberries, peaches and banana suspended in jellied vanilla yogurt—a refreshing twist on traditional jellied salads. Make this the night before to serve for breakfast or brunch.

Sliced fresh strawberries	1 cup	250 mL
Envelopes of unflavoured gelatin (1/4 oz., 7 g, each), about 4 1/2 tsp. (22 mL)	2	2
Reserved peach juice	1/2 cup	125 mL

(continued on next page)

Can of sliced peaches in juice, drained and juice reserved, chopped	28 oz.	796 mL
Vanilla yogurt	2 cups	500 mL
Diced banana	1 cup	250 mL

Arrange strawberries in bottom of plastic wrap-lined 9 x 5 x 3 inch (22 x 12.5 x 7.5 cm) loaf pan.

Sprinkle gelatin over peach juice in small saucepan. Let stand for 1 minute. Heat and stir on low until gelatin is dissolved. Cool to room temperature.

Combine remaining 3 ingredients in large bowl. Add gelatin mixture. Stir. Pour over strawberries. Chill, covered, for at least 6 hours or overnight until set. Invert onto cutting board. Discard plastic wrap. Cuts into 12 slices. Serves 6.

1 serving: 270 Calories; 1.5 g Total Fat (0.1 g Mono, 0.1 g Poly, 0.7 g Sat); 5 mg Cholesterol; 60 g Carbohydrate; 6 g Fibre; 7 g Protein; 73 mg Sodium

Tofu-ed Fruit Salad

Not just any old fruit salad—the mango dressing speckled with crunchy poppy seeds has tofu blended right in!

Package of peach-mango dessert tofu	5.35 oz.	150 g
Frozen mango pieces	1/3 cup	75 mL
Lemon juice	1 tsp.	5 mL
Liquid honey	1 tsp.	5 mL
Ground ginger	1/2 tsp.	2 mL
Poppy seeds	1 tsp.	5 mL
Cubed cantaloupe (3/4 inch, 2 cm, pieces)	2 cups	500 mL
Cubed honeydew (3/4 inch, 2 cm, pieces)	2 cups	500 mL
Sliced fresh strawberries	2 cups	500 mL
Green seedless grapes	1 cup	250 mL
Red seedless grapes	1 cup	250 mL

Process first 5 ingredients in blender until smooth. Transfer to large bowl.

Add poppy seeds. Stir. Add remaining 5 ingredients. Stir gently. Transfer to 4 serving bowls. Serves 4.

1 serving: 185 Calories; 1.7 g Total Fat (0.1 g Mono, 0.3 g Poly, 0.3 g Sat); 0 mg Cholesterol; 43 g Carbohydrate; 4 g Fibre; 4 g Protein; 31 mg Sodium

French Breakfast Salad

Citrus-kissed French toast croutons are tossed with fresh fruit in a sweet glaze.

Dry (or alcohol-free) white wine	1/2 cup	125 mL
Marmalade	1/2 cup	125 mL
Dried cranberries	1/2 cup	125 mL
Finely chopped dried figs	1/4 cup	60 mL
Can of sliced peaches in juice, drained, cut into 1 inch (2.5 cm) pieces	14 oz.	398 mL
Chopped unpeeled tart apple (such as Granny Smith)	1 cup	250 mL
Halved red grapes	1 cup	250 mL
Vanilla extract	1 tsp.	5 mL
Large oranges, segmented (see Tip, page 49, and Note)	2	2
FRENCH TOAST CROUTONS		
Large eggs	2	2
Vanilla yogurt	1/4 cup	60 mL
Granulated sugar	2 tbsp.	30 mL
Orange juice	2 tbsp.	30 mL
Grated orange zest	1 tsp.	5 mL
Texas bread slices	4	4
Butter (or hard margarine)	1 tbsp.	15 mL

Combine wine and marmalade in medium saucepan. Bring to a boil. Reduce heat to medium-low. Simmer, uncovered, for 10 minutes.

Add cranberries and figs. Stir. Simmer, uncovered, for about 5 minutes until cranberries are softened. Transfer to extra-large bowl. Cool.

Add next 5 ingredients. Stir.

French Toast Croutons: Whisk first 5 ingredients in large bowl. Dip 2 bread slices into egg mixture. Turn to coat both sides. Melt 1 1/2 tsp. (7 mL) butter in large frying pan on medium. Add bread. Cook for about 2 minutes per side until golden brown. Transfer to cutting board. Let stand until cool enough to handle. Cut into 1 inch (2.5 cm) pieces. Repeat with remaining bread, egg mixture and butter. Add to peach mixture. Toss gently. Serve immediately. Makes about 11 cups (2.75 L).

(continued on next page)

Fruit

1 1/2 cups (375 mL): 314 Calories; 4.0 g Total Fat (0.4 g Mono, 0.1 g Poly, 2.1 g Sat); 64 mg Cholesterol; 65 g Carbohydrate; 5 g Fibre; 5 g Protein; 167 mg Sodium

Note: Segment the orange over a small bowl to capture juice for the croutons.

Sunshine Salmon Salad

Bright and welcoming in flavour and colour, this salad is an elegant brunch option. The intense flavours of smoked salmon and citrus meld deliciously with creamy avocado.

Olive (or cooking) oil	1/4 cup	60 mL
Chopped fresh basil	2 tbsp.	30 mL
(or 1 1/2 tsp., 7 mL, dried)		
Orange juice	2 tbsp.	30 mL
White wine vinegar	2 tbsp.	30 mL
Sweet chili sauce	1 tbsp.	15 mL
Salt, just a pinch		
Chopped avocado (3/4 inch, 2 cm, pieces)	1 cup	250 mL
Thinly sliced red onion	1/4 cup	60 mL
Medium grapefruits, segmented	2	2
(see Tip, below)		
Medium oranges, segmented	2	2
(see Tip, below)		
Smoked salmon slices, cut into strips	4 oz.	113 g

Whisk first 6 ingredients in small bowl.

Arrange next 4 ingredients on 4 serving plates. Drizzle with dressing.

Top with salmon. Serves 4.

1 serving: 321 Calories; 20.8 Total Fat (14.3 g Mono, 3.0 g Poly, 3.1 g Sat); 7 mg Cholesterol; 33 g Carbohydrate; 12 g Fibre; 8 g Protein; 261 mg Sodium

Pictured on page 36.

 tip To segment citrus, trim a small slice of peel from both ends so the flesh is exposed. Place the fruit, bottom cut-side down, on a cutting board. Remove the peel with a sharp knife, cutting down and around the flesh, leaving as little pith as possible, over a small bowl, cut on either side of the membranes to release the segments.

Roasted Pear Salad

Balsamic-dressed pear pieces and shaved Parmesan lend an intriguing look to this light meal salad. Firm pears such as Bosc will give the best results.

Balsamic vinegar	1/3 cup	75 mL
Grated Parmesan cheese	3 tbsp.	50 mL
Cooking oil	2 tbsp.	30 mL
Finely chopped onion	2 tbsp.	30 mL
Pine nuts, toasted (see Tip, page 134)	2 tbsp.	30 mL
Liquid honey	1 tbsp.	15 mL
Dry mustard	1/2 tsp.	2 mL
Small firm, unpeeled pears	2	2
Arugula, lightly packed	10 cups	2.5 L
Pine nuts, toasted (see Tip, page 134)	1/3 cup	75 mL
Shaved Parmesan cheese	1/3 cup	75 mL

Process first 7 ingredients in blender or food processor until combined.

Cut each pear into quarters. Remove cores. Arrange, cut side-up, in single layer on foil-lined baking sheet with sides. Brush with 1/3 cup (75 mL) balsamic mixture. Broil on top rack in oven for 8 minutes. Transfer to cutting board. Let stand until cool enough to handle. Chop.

Toss remaining 3 ingredients in large bowl. Add remaining balsamic mixture. Toss. Scatter pear over top. Makes about 8 cups (2 L).

1 cup (250 mL): 157 Calories; 11 g Total Fat (3.5 g Mono, 3.8 g Poly, 2.2 g Sat); 8 mg Cholesterol; 11 g Carbohydrate; 2 g Fibre; 5 g Protein; 154 mg Sodium

 tip Too cold to barbecue? Use the broiler instead! Your food should cook in about the same length of time—and remember to turn or baste as directed. Set your oven rack so that the food is about 3 to 4 inches (7.5 to 10 cm) away from the top element—for most ovens, this is the top rack.

Sun-Dried Tomato Beef Salad

A combo of flavourful ingredients makes for a satisfying, Mediterranean-inspired meal. Salty olives and balsamic vinegar add a kick of flavour to complement wonderfully marinated steak.

Flank steak	1 lb.	454 g
Sun-dried tomato dressing	1/4 cup	60 mL
Water	16 cups	4 L
Salt	2 tsp.	10 mL
Fusilli pasta	4 cups	1 L
Sun-dried tomato dressing	1/2 cup	125 mL
Balsamic vinegar	2 tbsp.	30 mL
Fresh spinach leaves, lightly packed	1 cup	250 mL
Can of sliced black olives, drained	4 1/2 oz.	125 mL
Crumbled feta cheese	1/2 cup	125 mL
Sun-dried tomatoes in oil, blotted dry, chopped	1/4 cup	60 mL
Chopped fresh basil	2 tbsp.	30 mL

Pierce steak in several places with large fork. Place in medium shallow dish. Pour first amount of dressing over top. Turn until coated. Marinate, covered, in refrigerator for 1 hour, turning occasionally. Remove steak. Discard any remaining dressing. Preheat gas barbecue to medium-high (see Tip, page 50). Cook steak on greased grill for about 4 minutes per side until internal temperature reaches 145°F (63°C) for medium-rare or until steak reaches desired doneness. Transfer to cutting board. Cover with foil. Let stand for 10 minutes. Slice thinly across grain. Cut slices in half crosswise.

Combine water and salt in large pot. Bring to a boil. Add pasta. Boil, uncovered, for 7 to 9 minutes, stirring occasionally, until tender but firm. Drain. Rinse with cold water. Drain well. Transfer to large bowl.

Add second amount of dressing and vinegar to pasta. Toss.

Add remaining 5 ingredients and beef. Toss. Makes about 9 1/4 cups (2.3 L).

1 1/2 cups (375 mL): 432 Calories; 15.3 g Total Fat (4.6 g Mono, 0.6 g Poly, 4.7 g Sat); 39 mg Cholesterol; 48 g Carbohydrate; 3 g Fibre; 24 g Protein; 622 mg Sodium

Pictured on page 54.

Ham and Macaroni Salad

This is macaroni salad like you've never had it! This updated version of an old standby makes a fresh, light and colourful lunch for a summer's day.

Water	8 cups	2 L
Salt	1 tsp.	5 mL
Elbow macaroni	2 cups	500 mL
Chopped Black Forest ham	3/4 cup	175 mL
Chopped arugula (or fresh spinach leaves), lightly packed	1/2 cup	125 mL
Diced yellow pepper	1/2 cup	125 mL
Frozen tiny peas, thawed	1/2 cup	125 mL
Finely chopped red onion	2 tbsp.	30 mL
Raspberry vinaigrette dressing	1/2 cup	125 mL
Mayonnaise	2 tbsp.	30 mL
Poppy seeds	1/2 tsp.	2 mL
Grated Swiss cheese	1/3 cup	75 mL

Combine water and salt in large saucepan. Bring to a boil. Add pasta. Boil, uncovered, for 8 to 10 minutes, stirring occasionally, until tender but firm. Drain. Rinse with cold water. Drain well. Transfer to large bowl.

Add next 5 ingredients.

Whisk next 3 ingredients in small bowl. Add to pasta mixture. Toss.

Sprinkle with cheese. Toss. Makes about 6 cups (1.5 L).

1 cup (250 mL): 286 Calories; 12.2 g Total Fat (0 g Mono, trace Poly, 1.9 g Sat); 12 mg Cholesterol; 34 g Carbohydrate; 2 g Fibre; 10 g Protein; 335 mg Sodium

1. Scarlet Fruit Salad, page 40
2. Peppered Fruit Salad, page 43
3. Avocado Orange Salad, page 46

Props: Studio Nova

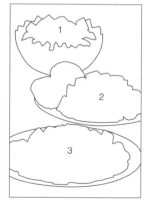

Perogy Salad

This colourful salad features a Ukrainian favourite—tasty perogies paired with a variety of traditional accompaniments such as sour cream and bacon. Cheese-filled ravioli or other stuffed pasta could be used in place of bite-sized perogies.

Water	8 cups	2 L
Bag of frozen bite-sized potato and Cheddar cheese perogies	2 lbs.	907 g
Baby spinach, lightly packed	1 cup	250 mL
Chopped English cucumber (with peel)	1 cup	250 mL
Sour cream	1/2 cup	125 mL
Wine sauerkraut, drained and finely chopped	1/2 cup	125 mL
Thinly sliced green onion	1/4 cup	60 mL
Chopped fresh dill (or 1/4 tsp., 1 mL, dried)	1 1/2 tsp.	7 mL
Bacon slices, cooked crisp and crumbled	4	4
Pepper, just a pinch		

Pour water into Dutch oven. Bring to a boil. Add perogies. Boil, uncovered, for about 5 minutes until tender. Drain. Rinse with cold water. Drain well.

Combine remaining 8 ingredients in large bowl. Add perogies. Toss. Makes about 7 cups (1.75 L).

1 cup (250 mL): 298 Calories; 6.6 g Total Fat (0.7 g Mono, 0.2 g Poly, 2.5 g Sat); 15 mg Cholesterol; 49 g Carbohydrate; 3 g Fibre; 9 g Protein; 616 mg Sodium

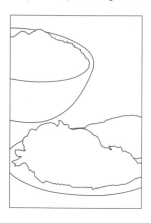

Sun-Dried Tomato Beef Salad, page 51

Props: H&H (House & Home)
        Studio Nova

Seafood Radiatore

Tender seafood makes a colourful and mild summer salad that's sure to please. The ridges of this uniquely-shaped pasta hold lots of sweet, creamy dressing for flavourful bites. Garnish with celery leaves and fresh dill sprigs.

Water	8 cups	2 L
Salt	1 tsp.	5 mL
Radiatore pasta	3 1/2 cups	875 mL
Broccoli florets	2 cups	500 mL
Coarsely chopped imitation crabmeat	2 cups	500 mL
Cooked salad shrimp	1 cup	250 mL
Thinly sliced celery	2/3 cup	150 mL
Grated carrot	1/2 cup	125 mL
Sliced green onion	1/2 cup	125 mL
CELERY DILL DRESSING		
Coleslaw dressing	1/2 cup	125 mL
Lemon juice	3 tbsp.	50 mL
Mayonnaise	2 tbsp.	30 mL
Chopped fresh dill	1 tbsp.	15 mL
(or 3/4 tsp., 4 mL, dried)		
Celery seed	1/2 tsp.	2 mL
Salt	1/4 tsp.	1 mL
Pepper	1/8 tsp.	0.5 mL

Combine water and salt in large saucepan. Bring to a boil. Add pasta. Boil, uncovered, for 6 minutes, stirring occasionally.

Add broccoli. Cook, uncovered, for about 1 minute, stirring occasionally, until pasta is tender but firm and broccoli is tender-crisp. Drain. Rinse with cold water. Drain well. Transfer to extra-large bowl.

Add next 5 ingredients. Toss.

Celery Dill Dressing: Combine all 7 ingredients in small bowl. Makes about 3/4 cup (175 mL). Add to pasta mixture. Toss. Makes about 12 cups (3 L).

1 1/2 cups (375 mL): 293 Calories; 12.2 g Total Fat (0.6 g Mono, 1.2 g Poly, 1.8 g Sat); 46 mg Cholesterol; 32 g Carbohydrate; 2 g Fibre; 12 g Protein; 281 mg Sodium

California Tortellini Salad

*This hearty, filling salad has real west-coast appeal: fresh seafood flavour,
tangy artichokes and a rich and creamy avocado dressing.*

Water	16 cups	4 L
Salt	2 tsp.	10 mL
Packages of fresh cheese tortellini (12 1/2 oz., 350 g, each)	2	2
Uncooked medium shrimp (peeled and deveined)	1 1/2 lbs.	680 g
Chopped red pepper	2 cups	500 mL
Jars of marinated artichoke hearts (6 oz., 170 mL, each), drained and chopped	2	2
Sliced green onion	1/2 cup	125 mL
AVOCADO MAYONNAISE DRESSING		
Chopped avocado	1 cup	250 mL
Mayonnaise	1/2 cup	125 mL
Lime juice	4 tsp.	20 mL
Garlic clove, minced (or 1/4 tsp., 1 mL, powder)	1	1
Salt	1/4 tsp.	1 mL
Pepper, sprinkle		

Combine water and salt in large pot. Bring to a boil. Add pasta. Boil, uncovered, for 5 minutes, stirring occasionally.

Add shrimp. Cook, uncovered, for about 2 minutes, stirring occasionally, until pasta is tender but firm and shrimp turn pink. Drain. Rinse with cold water. Drain well. Transfer to extra-large bowl.

Add next 3 ingredients.

Avocado Mayonnaise Dressing: Process all 6 ingredients in blender until smooth. Makes about 1 1/3 cups (325 mL). Add to pasta mixture. Stir. Makes about 14 cups (3.5 L).

1 1/2 cups (375 mL): 447 Calories; 18.5 g Total Fat (1.8 g Mono, 0.8 g Poly, 3.0 g Sat); 131 mg Cholesterol; 45 g Carbohydrate; 3 g Fibre; 25 g Protein; 350 mg Sodium

Rice Noodle Salad

Dig into this delicious salad full of rice noodles and veggies. The subtle Asian flavours in the peanutty dressing are fresh, and have a hint of spice.

Liquid honey	1 1/2 tbsp.	25 mL
Soy sauce	1 1/2 tbsp.	25 mL
Chili powder	1 tsp.	5 mL
Pork tenderloin, trimmed of fat, halved lengthwise	1	1
Water	8 cups	2 L
Medium rice stick noodles, broken in half	5 oz.	140 g
Diced English cucumber (with peel)	2 cups	500 mL
Chopped tomato	1 cup	250 mL
Pine nuts, toasted (see Tip, page 134)	2/3 cup	150 mL
PEANUT GINGER DRESSING		
Peanut (or cooking) oil	3 tbsp.	50 mL
Rice vinegar	3 tbsp.	50 mL
Smooth peanut butter	2 tbsp.	30 mL
Sweet chili sauce	2 tbsp.	30 mL
Soy sauce	2 tsp.	10 mL
Finely grated ginger root (or 1/4 tsp., 1 mL, powder)	1 tsp.	5 mL
Garlic clove, minced (or 1/4 tsp., 1 mL, powder)	1	1
Salt, sprinkle		
Pepper, sprinkle		

Combine first 3 ingredients in small bowl. Brush over tenderloin. Preheat gas barbecue to medium (see Tip, page 50). Cook tenderloin on greased grill for 4 to 5 minutes per side until internal temperature reaches 155°F (68°C). Transfer to cutting board. Cover with foil. Let stand for 10 minutes. Internal temperature should rise to at least 160°F (71°C). Slice thinly. Cover to keep warm.

Pour water into large saucepan. Bring to a boil. Add noodles. Boil, uncovered, for about 5 minutes, stirring occasionally, until tender but firm. Drain. Rinse with cold water. Drain well. Transfer to large bowl.

Add next 3 ingredients and pork. Toss.

(continued on next page)

Peanut Ginger Dressing: Process all 9 ingredients in blender until smooth. Makes about 2/3 cup (150 mL). Add to noodle mixture. Toss. Makes about 7 1/2 cups (1.9 L).

1 cup (250 mL): 324 Calories; 18.1 g Total Fat (5.9 g Mono, 6.2 g Poly, 2.8 g Sat); 36 mg Cholesterol; 26 g Carbohydrate; 1 g Fibre; 16 g Protein; 503 mg Sodium

Beefy Blue Pasta Salad

Put leftover roast beef to good use in this simple, rich and creamy pasta salad. If time is short, substitute ready-made blue cheese dressing for this homemade version.

Water	8 cups	2 L
Salt	1 tsp.	5 mL
Medium shell pasta	2 cups	500 mL
Broccoli florets	1 cup	250 mL
Chopped cooked roast beef	1 cup	250 mL
Julienned red pepper	1/2 cup	125 mL
Julienned yellow pepper	1/2 cup	125 mL
Thinly sliced leek (white part only), halved lengthwise before slicing	1/4 cup	60 mL
CREAMY BLUE CHEESE DRESSING		
Crumbled blue cheese	1/4 cup	60 mL
Mayonnaise	1/4 cup	60 mL
Sour cream	1/4 cup	60 mL
Chopped green onion	1 tbsp.	15 mL
Lime juice	1 tbsp.	15 mL
Salt, just a pinch		
Pepper, just a pinch		

Combine water and salt in large saucepan. Bring to a boil. Add pasta. Boil, uncovered, for 8 to 10 minutes, stirring occasionally, until tender but firm. Drain. Rinse with cold water. Drain well. Transfer to large bowl.

Add next 5 ingredients. Toss.

Creamy Blue Cheese Dressing: Combine all 7 ingredients in small bowl. Makes about 3/4 cup (175 mL). Add to pasta mixture. Toss. Makes about 6 cups (1.5 L).

1 cup (250 mL): 252 Calories; 12.0 g Total Fat (0.4 g Mono, 0.1 g Poly, 3.5 g Sat); 27 mg Cholesterol; 25 g Carbohydrate; 2 g Fibre; 11 g Protein; 268 mg Sodium

Hazelnut Halibut Pasta Salad

Pull out all the stops with this guest-worthy dish—appetizing halibut croutons rest atop a light pasta salad, all dressed in an orange balsamic vinaigrette.

Water	8 cups	2 L
Salt	1 tsp.	5 mL
Small shell pasta	2 1/2 cups	625 mL
Fresh spinach leaves, lightly packed	4 cups	1 L
Chopped tomato	1 cup	250 mL
Liquid honey	1/3 cup	75 mL
Orange juice	1/3 cup	75 mL
Dijon mustard	1/4 cup	60 mL
Balsamic vinegar	2 tbsp.	30 mL
Pepper	1/4 tsp.	1 mL
HALIBUT CROUTONS		
Large egg, fork-beaten	1	1
Salt	1/8 tsp.	0.5 mL
Pepper	1/8 tsp.	0.5 mL
Flaked hazelnuts (filberts), toasted, finely chopped (see Tip, page 134)	1 cup	250 mL
Halibut fillets, any small bones removed, cut into 1 inch (2.5 cm) pieces	3/4 lb.	340 g

Combine water and salt in large saucepan. Bring to a boil. Add pasta. Boil, uncovered, for 8 to 10 minutes, stirring occasionally, until tender but firm. Drain. Rinse with cold water. Drain well. Transfer to large bowl. Add spinach and tomato.

Whisk next 5 ingredients in small bowl. Add to pasta mixture. Toss.

Halibut Croutons: Combine first 3 ingredients in small bowl. Place hazelnuts in small shallow dish.

Dip fish into egg mixture. Press into hazelnuts until coated. Discard any remaining egg mixture and hazelnuts. Arrange on greased baking sheet with sides. Bake in 400°F (205°C) oven for about 5 minutes until fish flakes easily when tested with fork. Let stand until cool. Makes about 24 halibut croutons. Spoon pasta mixture onto serving platter. Arrange Halibut Croutons over top. Serves 4.

(continued on next page)

1 serving: 509 Calories; 17.2 g Total Fat (10.5 g Mono, 2.4 g Poly, 1.6 g Sat); 68 mg Cholesterol; 62 g Carbohydrate; 3 g Fibre; 28 g Protein; 336 mg Sodium

Pictured on page 72.

Seafood Gazpacho Salad

The herb-fresh flavours of the classic soup are transformed into a meal salad.
Oodles of orzo are tossed with tasty seafood and crisp veggies.

Water	8 cups	2 L
Salt	1 tsp.	5 mL
Orzo	2 cups	500 mL
Small bay scallops	1 lb.	454 g
Can of diced tomatoes, drained	14 oz.	398 mL
Cooked salad shrimp	1 1/2 cups	375 mL
Diced English cucumber (with peel)	1 cup	250 mL
Olive oil	3 tbsp.	50 mL
Lemon juice	2 tbsp.	30 mL
Red wine vinegar	2 tbsp.	30 mL
Chopped fresh cilantro (or parsley)	1 tbsp.	15 mL
Liquid honey	1 tbsp.	15 mL
Chopped fresh basil (or 1/4 tsp., 1 mL, dried)	1 tsp.	5 mL
Ground cumin	1/2 tsp.	2 mL
Salt	3/4 tsp.	4 mL
Pepper	1/2 tsp.	2 mL

Combine water and salt in Dutch oven. Bring to a boil. Add pasta. Boil, uncovered, for 7 minutes, stirring occasionally.

Add scallops. Cook, uncovered, for about 2 minutes, stirring occasionally, until pasta is tender but firm and scallops are opaque. Drain. Rinse with cold water. Drain well. Transfer to large bowl.

Add next 3 ingredients.

Whisk remaining 9 ingredients in small bowl. Add to pasta mixture. Stir. Makes about 9 1/2 cups (2.4 L).

1 1/2 cups (375 mL): 413 Calories; 11.9 g Total Fat (5.9 g Mono, 3.2 g Poly, 1.6 g Sat); 73 mg Cholesterol; 48 g Carbohydrate; 3 g Fibre; 25 g Protein; 634 mg Sodium

Noodle Bowl Salad

Vietnamese bun *(boon) is a refreshingly satisfying individual noodle salad.
To take for lunch, pack the salad and dressing separately.*

Fish sauce	6 tbsp.	100 mL
Granulated sugar	1/4 cup	60 mL
Lime juice	1/4 cup	60 mL
Chili paste (sambal oelek)	1 1/2 tsp.	7 mL
Garlic cloves, minced	2	2
Water	2 tbsp.	30 mL
Grated carrot	2 tbsp.	30 mL
Beef strip loin steak	1/2 lb.	225 g
Rice vermicelli	4 oz.	113 g
Shredded iceberg lettuce, lightly packed	2 cups	500 mL
Fresh bean sprouts	1/2 cup	125 mL
Julienned English cucumber (with peel)	1/2 cup	125 mL
Coarsely chopped unsalted peanuts	1/4 cup	60 mL
Chopped fresh basil	2 tbsp.	30 mL
Chopped fresh mint	2 tbsp.	30 mL

Stir first 5 ingredients in small bowl until sugar is dissolved. Reserve 1/4 cup
(60 mL).

Add water and carrot to remaining fish sauce mixture. Chill.

Place steak in medium shallow bowl. Pour reserved fish sauce mixture over
top. Turn until coated. Marinate, covered, in refrigerator for 1 hour. Remove
steak. Discard any remaining fish sauce mixture. Preheat gas barbecue to
medium-high (see Tip, page 50). Cook steak on greased grill for about
3 minutes per side until internal temperature reaches 145°F (63°C) for
medium rare or until steak reaches desired doneness. Transfer to cutting
board. Cover with foil. Let stand for 10 minutes. Slice thinly.

Place vermicelli in large heatproof bowl. Cover with boiling water. Let stand
for about 5 minutes until tender. Drain. Rinse with cold water. Drain well.

Toss remaining 6 ingredients in large bowl. Transfer to 2 serving bowls.
Arrange noodles over top. Top with beef. Drizzle chilled fish sauce mixture
over beef. Toss. Serves 2.

*1 serving: 775 Calories; 34.9 g Total Fat (15.6 g Mono, 3.9 g Poly, 11.6 g Sat); 76 mg Cholesterol;
82 g Carbohydrate; 5 g Fibre; 35 g Protein; 2944 mg Sodium*

Asiago Beef and Bow Ties

Asiago cheese lends its delicious sharpness to this creamy salad with fresh tomato and asparagus. The shape and colour contrasts make this an attractive option when company pops by for lunch.

Water	8 cups	2 L
Salt	1 tsp.	5 mL
Medium bow pasta	2 cups	500 mL
Chopped fresh asparagus	1 1/2 cups	375 mL
Chopped deli shaved beef (or minced cooked roast beef)	2 cups	500 mL
Grape tomatoes	1 cup	250 mL
Sliced green onion	1/4 cup	60 mL
CREAMY ASIAGO DRESSING		
Grated Asiago cheese	1/2 cup	125 mL
Sour cream	1/4 cup	60 mL
White wine vinegar	2 tbsp.	30 mL
Cooking oil	1 tbsp.	15 mL
Salt	1/4 tsp.	1 mL
Pepper	1/4 tsp.	1 mL

Combine water and salt in Dutch oven. Bring to a boil. Add pasta. Boil, uncovered, for 9 minutes, stirring occasionally.

Add asparagus. Cook, uncovered, for 4 to 5 minutes, stirring occasionally, until pasta is tender but firm and asparagus is tender-crisp. Drain. Rinse with cold water. Drain well. Transfer to large bowl.

Add next 3 ingredients.

Creamy Asiago Dressing: Combine all 6 ingredients in small bowl. Makes about 1/2 cup (125 mL). Add to pasta mixture. Toss. Chill for 2 hours to blend flavours. Makes about 8 cups (2 L).

1 cup (250 mL): 178 Calories; 6.6 g Total Fat (1.0 g Mono, 0.5 g Poly, 2.6 g Sat); 27 mg Cholesterol; 18 g Carbohydrate; 2 g Fibre; 11 g Protein; 302 mg Sodium

Greek Pork Pasta Salad

This hearty pasta salad is loaded with Greek flavours, including souvlaki-spiced pork and a feta dressing. The dressing can be made ahead and refrigerated until ready to use.

Cooking oil	1 tsp.	5 mL
Boneless pork shoulder butt steak, trimmed of fat and cut into 3/4 inch (2 cm) cubes	3/4 lb.	340 g
Greek seasoning	1 tbsp.	15 mL
Water	8 cups	2 L
Salt	1 tsp.	5 mL
Fusilli	1 1/2 cups	375 mL
Chopped English cucumber (with peel)	1 cup	250 mL
Halved cherry tomatoes	1 cup	250 mL
Chopped red onion	1/2 cup	125 mL
Chopped red pepper	1/2 cup	125 mL
Pitted whole black olives	1/2 cup	125 mL
Salt	3/4 tsp.	4 mL
Pepper	1/4 tsp.	1 mL
GREEK FETA DRESSING		
Plain yogurt	1/2 cup	125 mL
Crumbled feta cheese	1/4 cup	60 mL
Greek seasoning	1/2 tsp.	2 mL

Heat cooking oil in large frying pan on medium-high. Add pork. Sprinkle with Greek seasoning. Cook for about 8 minutes, stirring occasionally, until no longer pink inside. Cool.

Combine water and salt in large saucepan. Bring to a boil. Add pasta. Boil, uncovered, for 7 to 9 minutes, stirring occasionally, until tender but firm. Drain. Rinse with cold water. Drain well. Transfer to large bowl.

Add next 7 ingredients and pork. Toss.

Greek Feta Dressing: Combine all 3 ingredients in small bowl. Makes about 2/3 cup (150 mL). Add to pasta mixture. Toss. Makes about 8 cups (2 L).

1 cup (250 mL): 177 Calories; 7.3 g Total Fat (3.1 g Mono, 0.7 g Poly, 2.6 g Sat); 31 mg Cholesterol; 17 g Carbohydrate; 1 g Fibre; 11 g Protein; 382 mg Sodium

Pictured on page 72.

Shrimp Rotini Primavera

The fresh veggies, juicy tomatoes and baby shrimp in this garlicky pasta salad make for great picnic fare. Try it chilled for a more mellowed flavour.

Water	8 cups	2 L
Salt	1 tsp.	5 mL
Rotini pasta	3 cups	750 mL
Cooked salad shrimp	2 cups	500 mL
Cherry tomatoes, halved	1 cup	250 mL
Diced zucchini (with peel)	1 cup	250 mL
Frozen tiny peas, thawed	1 cup	250 mL
Finely chopped red onion	1/4 cup	60 mL
Olive (or cooking) oil	1/4 cup	60 mL
Red wine vinegar	3 tbsp.	50 mL
Grated Parmesan cheese	2 tbsp.	30 mL
Lemon juice	1 tbsp.	15 mL
Salt	1/2 tsp.	2 mL
Pepper	1/2 tsp.	2 mL
Small garlic clove, minced	1	1
(or 1/8 tsp., 0.5 mL, powder)		

Combine water and salt in large saucepan. Bring to a boil. Add pasta. Boil, uncovered, for 12 to 14 minutes, stirring occasionally, until tender but firm. Drain. Rinse with cold water. Drain well. Transfer to large bowl.

Add next 5 ingredients. Toss.

Whisk remaining 7 ingredients in small bowl. Add to pasta mixture. Toss. Serve immediately or chill. Makes about 8 cups (2 L).

1 cup (250 mL): 262 Calories; 12.4 g Total Fat (6.1 g Mono, 3.1 g Poly, 2.1 g Sat); 53 mg Cholesterol; 26 g Carbohydrate; 3 g Fibre; 12 g Protein; 309 mg Sodium

Paré Pointer

When an Irish potato travels, he becomes a French fry.

Layered Moroccan Salad

Colourful ingredients offer sweet flavours and pleasing textures. Arrange the sliced vegetables to show through a clear glass dish for pretty presentation.

Prepared chicken broth	1 1/2 cups	375 mL
Box of roasted garlic and olive oil couscous	7 oz.	198 g
Mayonnaise	1 cup	250 mL
Plain yogurt	1 cup	250 mL
Chopped fresh mint	1/4 cup	60 mL
Chopped fresh parsley	1/4 cup	60 mL
Liquid honey	2 tbsp.	30 mL
Ground cumin	1 tbsp.	15 mL
Ground cinnamon	1 tsp.	5 mL
Salt	1/2 tsp.	2 mL
Pepper	1/8 tsp.	0.5 mL
Can of lentils, rinsed and drained	19 oz.	540 mL
Shredded romaine lettuce, lightly packed	2 cups	500 mL
Thinly sliced carrot	2 cups	500 mL
Sliced English cucumber (with peel)	2 cups	500 mL
Halved cherry tomatoes	2 cups	500 mL
Chopped cooked chicken (see Tip, page 41)	2 cups	500 mL
Chopped dried apricot	1/2 cup	125 mL
Chopped dried cranberries	1/2 cup	125 mL
Chopped pistachios	1/2 cup	125 mL

Measure broth into medium saucepan. Bring to a boil. Add couscous. Stir. Remove from heat. Let stand, covered, for about 5 minutes until liquid is absorbed. Fluff with fork. Transfer to extra-large glass bowl. Chill, uncovered, for about 30 minutes until cold.

Combine next 9 ingredients in medium bowl.

Add lentils and 1 cup (250 mL) mayonnaise mixture to couscous. Stir. Layer next 5 ingredients, in order given, over couscous mixture. Spread remaining mayonnaise mixture over chicken.

(continued on next page)

Pasta & Noodles

Scatter remaining 3 ingredients over top. Makes about 16 cups (4 L).

1 1/2 cups (375 mL): 432 Calories; 22.1 g Total Fat (2.2 g Mono, 1.4 g Poly, 3.4 g Sat); 33 mg Cholesterol; 41 g Carbohydrate; 8 g Fibre; 17 g Protein; 733 mg Sodium

Pictured on page 71.

Lemony Angel Salad

A bright springtime pasta salad with toasty pine nuts, arugula and juicy tomato tossed with angel hair pasta. Serve as a light lunch, or as a first course with a heavier meat dish, Italian-style.

Water	12 cups	3 L
Salt	1 1/2 tsp.	7 mL
Angel hair pasta, broken in half	8 oz.	225 g
Olive oil	2 tbsp.	30 mL
Garlic cloves, minced	2	2
Lemon juice	2 tbsp.	30 mL
White balsamic (or white wine) vinegar	2 tbsp.	30 mL
Grated lemon zest	1 tsp.	5 mL
Chopped seeded Roma (plum) tomato	1 cup	250 mL
Shredded arugula, lightly packed	1 cup	250 mL
Grated Asiago cheese	1/2 cup	125 mL
Pine nuts, toasted (see Tip, page 134)	1/2 cup	125 mL
Sliced green onion	1/2 cup	125 mL

Combine water and salt in Dutch oven. Bring to a boil. Add pasta. Boil, uncovered, for 3 to 5 minutes, stirring occasionally, until tender but firm. Drain. Rinse with cold water. Drain well. Transfer to large bowl.

Heat olive oil in medium frying pan on medium. Add garlic. Heat and stir for about 30 seconds until fragrant. Remove from heat. Add next 3 ingredients. Stir. Add to pasta.

Add remaining 5 ingredients to pasta mixture. Toss. Makes about 7 cups (1.75 L).

1 cup (250 mL): 260 Calories; 13.8 g Total Fat (4.7 g Mono, 3.9 g Poly, 2.5 g Sat); 7 mg Cholesterol; 27 g Carbohydrate; 1 g Fibre; 7 g Protein; 81 mg Sodium

Kibbutz Salad

This refreshing meal salad features Middle-Eastern-inspired ingredients such as chickpeas, couscous and citrus. Dried thyme, sesame seeds and cranberry mimic the flavour of za'atar, a traditional blend of sesame, herbs and spices.

Water	1 3/4 cups	425 mL
Whole-wheat couscous	1 cup	250 mL
Dried cranberries, finely chopped	1/4 cup	60 mL
Can of chickpeas (garbanzo beans), rinsed and drained	14 oz.	398 mL
Diced English cucumber (with peel)	1/2 cup	125 mL
Diced tomato	1/2 cup	125 mL
Diced fennel bulb (white part only)	1/4 cup	60 mL
Chopped fresh mint	1 tbsp.	15 mL
Chopped fresh parsley	1 tbsp.	15 mL
Lemon juice	1/4 cup	60 mL
Olive (or cooking) oil	2 tbsp.	30 mL
Sesame seeds, toasted (see Tip, page 134)	2 tsp.	10 mL
Salt	3/4 tsp.	4 mL
Coarsely ground pepper	1/2 tsp.	2 mL
Dried thyme	1/2 tsp.	2 mL
Garlic clove, minced (or 1/4 tsp., 1 mL, powder)	1	1

Pour water into medium saucepan. Bring to a boil. Add couscous and cranberries. Stir. Remove from heat. Let stand, covered, for about 5 minutes until liquid is absorbed. Fluff with fork. Transfer to large bowl. Let stand until cool.

Add next 6 ingredients. Toss.

Whisk remaining 7 ingredients in small bowl. Add to couscous mixture. Toss. Makes about 8 cups (2 L).

1 cup (250 mL): 148 Calories; 4.9 g Total Fat (2.7 g Mono, 0.9 g Poly, 0.5 g Sat); 0 mg Cholesterol; 23 g Carbohydrate; 4 g Fibre; 5 g Protein; 274 mg Sodium

Satay Pork Pasta

A refreshingly different choice for the potluck, infused with ginger and peanut flavours. Crisp peppers and snow peas contrast with tender pork and rotini.

Pork tenderloin, trimmed of fat and cut into thin slices	3/4 lb.	340 g
Cooking oil	2 tsp.	10 mL
Water	12 cups	3 L
Salt	1 1/2 tsp.	7 mL
Rotini pasta	3 1/2 cups	875 mL
Slivered red pepper	1 cup	250 mL
Sliced trimmed snow peas	1 cup	250 mL
Grated carrot	1/2 cup	125 mL
Chopped green onion	1/3 cup	75 mL
Sesame seeds, toasted (see Tip, page 134)	2 tbsp.	30 mL
Salad dressing (or mayonnaise)	1/2 cup	125 mL
Smooth peanut butter	1 tbsp.	15 mL
Soy sauce	2 tsp.	10 mL
Chili paste (sambal oelek)	1 tsp.	5 mL
Finely grated ginger root (or 1/4 tsp., 1 mL, powder)	1 tsp.	5 mL

Cut pork slices into thin strips. Heat large frying pan or wok on medium-high until very hot. Add cooking oil. Add pork. Stir-fry for about 5 minutes until no longer pink. Cool.

Combine water and salt in Dutch oven. Bring to a boil. Add pasta. Boil, uncovered, for 12 to 14 minutes, stirring occasionally, until tender but firm. Drain. Rinse with cold water. Drain well. Transfer to large bowl.

Add next 5 ingredients and pork.

Whisk remaining 5 ingredients in small bowl until smooth. Add to pasta mixture. Toss. Makes about 9 cups (2.25 L).

1 cup (250 mL): 235 Calories; 9.1 g Total Fat (2.4 g Mono, 2.8 g Poly, 1.4 g Sat); 28 mg Cholesterol; 25 g Carbohydrate; 2 g Fibre; 13 g Protein; 234 mg Sodium

Noodle Salad Wraps

Rice noodles are kicked up a notch with crunchy veggies and a sweet and spicy dressing. The lettuce "lining" helps keep your tortilla wraps from getting soggy before lunch!

Broccoli slaw (or shredded cabbage with carrot), lightly packed	1/2 cup	125 mL
Chopped cooked chicken (see Tip, page 41)	1/2 cup	125 mL
Asian-style sesame dressing	1/4 cup	60 mL
Water	6 cups	1.5 L
Small rice stick noodles, broken in half	1 oz.	28 g
Butter lettuce leaves	4	4
Flour tortillas (9 inch, 22 cm, diameter)	2	2

Combine first 3 ingredients in medium bowl.

Pour water into large saucepan. Bring to a boil. Add noodles. Boil, uncovered, for about 5 minutes, stirring occasionally, until tender but firm. Drain. Rinse with cold water. Drain well. Add to chicken mixture. Toss until coated.

Place 2 lettuce leaves over 1 tortilla. Arrange 1/2 cup (125 mL) noodle mixture across centre of lettuce. Fold sides over filling. Roll up from bottom to enclose filling. Repeat with remaining lettuce leaves, tortilla and noodle mixture. Makes 2 salad wraps.

1 salad wrap: 354 Calories; 13.8 g Total Fat (0.8 g Mono, 0.5 g Poly, 1.6 g Sat); 33 mg Cholesterol; 41 g Carbohydrate; 1 g Fibre; 17 g Protein; 695 mg Sodium

1. Layered Moroccan Salad, page 66
2. Aussie Burger Salad, page 38

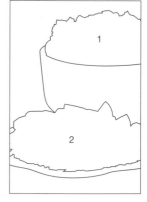

Italian Wedding Salad

The classic flavours of Italian Wedding Soup lend themselves to a hearty and colourful meal salad. The small pasta shells hold lentils and diced morsels perfectly, with the salami adding a salty sharpness.

Water	8 cups	2 L
Salt	1 tsp.	5 mL
Tiny shell pasta	2 1/2 cups	625 mL
Can of lentils, rinsed and drained	19 oz.	540 mL
Sun-dried tomato dressing	3/4 cup	175 mL
Jar of marinated artichoke hearts, drained and chopped	6 oz.	170 mL
Diced mozzarella cheese	2/3 cup	150 mL
Diced red pepper	2/3 cup	150 mL
Diced salami slices	2/3 cup	150 mL
Diced celery	1/2 cup	125 mL
Sliced green onion	1/4 cup	60 mL
Chopped fresh parsley, for garnish	2 tbsp.	30 mL

Combine water and salt in large saucepan. Bring to a boil. Add pasta. Boil, uncovered, for 8 to 10 minutes, stirring occasionally, until tender but firm. Drain. Rinse with cold water. Drain well. Transfer to large bowl.

Add next 8 ingredients. Toss.

Garnish with parsley. Makes about 8 cups (2 L).

1 cup (250 mL): 252 Calories; 9.1 g Total Fat (1.6 g Mono, 0.3 g Poly, 1.9 g Sat); 12 mg Cholesterol; 31 g Carbohydrate; 6 g Fibre; 13 g Protein; 707 mg Sodium

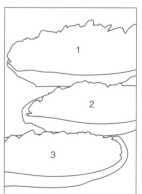

1. Hazelnut Halibut Pasta Salad, page 60
2. Sesame Chicken Noodle Salad, page 74
3. Greek Pork Pasta Salad, page 64

Props: Moderno

Sesame Chicken Noodle Salad

Who needs takeout? Brightly coloured and appealing with peppers and egg noodles, this Asian-style chicken salad is delicious with a sesame dressing.

Chinese dried mushrooms	4	4
Boiling water	1 cup	250 mL
Water	8 cups	2 L
Fresh, thin Chinese-style egg noodles	8 oz.	225 g
Shredded fresh spinach leaves, lightly packed	1 cup	250 mL
Asian-style sesame dressing	1/2 cup	125 mL
Grated carrot	1/2 cup	125 mL
Slivered red pepper	1/2 cup	125 mL
Sliced green onion	1/4 cup	60 mL
Sesame oil (for flavour)	1 tsp.	5 mL
Sesame (or olive) oil	1 tsp.	5 mL
Boneless, skinless chicken thighs, cut into 1/2 inch (12 mm) pieces	3/4 lb.	340 g
Dried crushed chilies	1/8 tsp.	0.5 mL
Sesame seeds, toasted (see Tip, page 134)	1 tbsp.	15 mL

Combine mushrooms and boiling water in small heatproof bowl. Let stand for about 20 minutes until softened. Drain. Remove and discard stems. Slice thinly.

Pour water into large saucepan. Bring to a boil. Add noodles. Boil, uncovered, for about 30 seconds until tender but firm. Drain. Rinse with cold water. Drain well. Transfer to cutting board. Chop once or twice. Transfer to large bowl.

Add next 6 ingredients and mushrooms. Toss.

Heat large frying pan or wok on medium-high until very hot. Add second amount of sesame oil. Add chicken. Sprinkle with chilies. Stir-fry for about 3 minutes until no longer pink inside. Add to noodle mixture. Toss.

Sprinkle with sesame seeds. Makes about 7 1/2 cups (1.9 L).

1 cup (250 mL): 283 Calories; 13.9 g Total Fat (3.3 g Mono, 5.3 g Poly, 2.5 g Sat); 61 mg Cholesterol; 26 g Carbohydrate; 2 g Fibre; 14 g Protein; 206 mg Sodium

Pictured on page 72.

Rice-Wrapped Noodle Salad

Tofu and peanut transform these inviting salad wraps from a favourite appetizer to a delicious and portable meal! Wrap well to take along for lunch or a picnic.

Peanut sauce	1/2 cup	125 mL
Lime juice	2 tbsp.	30 mL
Granulated sugar	1 tbsp.	15 mL
Chili paste (sambal oelek)	1 tsp.	5 mL
Package of firm tofu, diced	12 1/4 oz.	350 g
Rice vermicelli, broken up	3 oz.	85 g
Diced English cucumber (with peel)	1 cup	250 mL
Grated carrot	1 cup	250 mL
Coarsely chopped dry-roasted peanuts	1/2 cup	125 mL
Chopped fresh cilantro	1/4 cup	60 mL
Rice paper rounds (9 inch, 22 cm, diameter)	12	12

Combine first 4 ingredients in large bowl.

Add tofu. Stir until coated. Chill, covered, for 30 minutes to blend flavours.

Place vermicelli in medium heatproof bowl. Cover with boiling water. Let stand for about 5 minutes until tender. Drain. Rinse with cold water. Drain well. Add to tofu mixture.

Add next 4 ingredients. Toss.

Place 1 rice paper round in shallow bowl of hot water until just softened. Place on work surface. Spoon about 1/2 cup (125 mL) vermicelli mixture in centre. Fold sides over filling. Roll up tightly from bottom to enclose filling. Repeat with remaining rice paper rounds and vermicelli mixture. Makes 12 salad wraps.

1 salad wrap: 141 Calories; 6.2 g Total Fat (2.8 g Mono, 1.9 g Poly, 1.1 g Sat); 0 mg Cholesterol; 18 g Carbohydrate; 1 g Fibre; 5 g Protein; 158 mg Sodium

Paré Pointer

Any animal can fly higher than a house. Houses can't fly.

Mediterranean Chicken Salad

Get all the sun-drenched flavours of the Mediterranean without a plane ticket! Tender orzo absorbs all the rich tomato and olive flavours in the dressing for a bright, tangy meal salad.

Water	8 cups	2 L
Salt	1 tsp.	5 mL
Orzo	1 cup	250 mL
Chopped cooked chicken (see Tip, page 41)	1 1/2 cups	375 mL
Sun-dried tomatoes in oil, blotted dry, finely chopped	2 tbsp.	30 mL
Olive oil	1/3 cup	75 mL
Red wine vinegar	1/4 cup	60 mL
Tomato paste (see Tip, below)	1 tbsp.	15 mL
Granulated sugar	1/2 tsp.	2 mL
Quartered cherry tomatoes	1 cup	250 mL
Jar of marinated artichokes, drained and chopped	6 oz.	170 mL
Coarsely chopped pitted kalamata olives	1/2 cup	125 mL
Currants	1/4 cup	60 mL
Capers (optional)	2 tbsp.	30 mL

Combine water and salt in large saucepan. Bring to a boil. Add pasta. Boil, uncovered, for 8 to 10 minutes, stirring occasionally, until tender but firm. Drain. Rinse with cold water. Drain well. Transfer to large bowl.

Add chicken and sun-dried tomato.

Whisk next 4 ingredients in small bowl. Add to pasta mixture. Stir.

Add remaining 5 ingredients. Stir. Chill for 30 minutes to blend flavours. Makes about 6 cups (1.5 L).

1 cup (250 mL): 330 Calories; 18.5 g Total Fat (10.9 g Mono, 2.6 g Poly, 2.7 g Sat); 31 mg Cholesterol; 27 g Carbohydrate; 3 g Fibre; 15 g Protein; 244 mg Sodium

 tip If a recipe calls for less than an entire can of tomato paste, freeze the unopened can for 30 minutes. Open both ends and push the contents through one end. Slice off only what you need. Freeze the remaining paste in a resealable freezer bag or plastic wrap for future use.

Fusilli Chicken Salad

A salad with a fresh appearance—the use of broccoli slaw gives you all the nutrition with a different look than florets. The rich, smoky dressing evenly coats tender fusilli and chicken bites.

Water	12 cups	3 L
Salt	1 1/2 tsp.	7 mL
Fusilli pasta	3 cups	750 mL
Broccoli slaw (or shredded cabbage with carrot), lightly packed	1 1/2 cups	375 mL
Chopped cooked chicken (see Tip, page 41)	1 1/2 cups	375 mL
Sliced fresh white mushrooms	1 cup	250 mL
Chopped red onion	1/4 cup	60 mL
CREAMY BACON DRESSING		
Bacon slices, cooked crisp and crumbled	6	6
Buttermilk	2/3 cup	150 mL
Chopped fresh parsley	6 tbsp.	100 mL
Cooking oil	6 tbsp.	100 mL
White wine vinegar	1/4 cup	60 mL
Grated Parmesan cheese	2 tbsp.	30 mL
Dijon mustard	1 1/2 tbsp.	25 mL
Granulated sugar	4 tsp.	20 mL
Garlic cloves, halved	2	2
Salt	1/4 tsp.	1 mL
Pepper	1/4 tsp.	1 mL

Combine water and salt in Dutch oven. Bring to a boil. Add pasta. Boil, uncovered, for 7 to 9 minutes, stirring occasionally, until tender but firm. Drain. Rinse with cold water. Drain well. Transfer to large bowl.

Add next 4 ingredients.

Creamy Bacon Dressing: Process all 11 ingredients in blender until smooth. Makes about 1 1/2 cups (375 mL). Add to pasta mixture. Toss. Makes about 9 cups (2.25 L).

1 cup (250 mL): 288 Calories; 14.3 g Total Fat (6.9 g Mono, 3.3 g Poly, 2.3 g Sat); 29 mg Cholesterol; 26 g Carbohydrate; 2 g Fibre; 14 g Protein; 266 mg Sodium

Chicken Fajita Salad

This hearty penne salad packs all the flavour of your favourite fajitas with chili heat, barbecued chicken and sautéed veggies.

Water	8 cups	2 L
Salt	1 tsp.	5 mL
Penne pasta	2 cups	500 mL
Boneless, skinless chicken breast halves	3/4 lb.	340 g
Barbecue sauce	2 tbsp.	30 mL
Cooking oil	1 tbsp.	15 mL
Ground cumin	1 tsp.	5 mL
Dried crushed chilies	1/4 tsp.	1 mL
Thinly sliced green pepper	1 cup	250 mL
Thinly sliced onion	1 cup	250 mL
Thinly sliced red pepper	1 cup	250 mL
Frozen kernel corn	1/2 cup	125 mL
Barbecue sauce	1/4 cup	60 mL
Sour cream	1/4 cup	60 mL
Lime juice	2 tsp.	10 mL
Salt	1/4 tsp.	1 mL
Thinly sliced green onion	3 tbsp.	50 mL

Combine water and salt in large saucepan. Bring to a boil. Add pasta. Boil, uncovered, for 14 to 16 minutes, stirring occasionally, until tender but firm. Drain. Rinse with cold water. Drain well. Transfer to large bowl.

Brush both sides of chicken breasts with first amount of barbecue sauce. Arrange on greased baking sheet with sides. Bake in 375°F (190°C) oven for about 9 minutes per side until internal temperature reaches 170°F (77°C). Transfer to cutting board. Let stand until cool. Slice thinly. Add to pasta.

Heat cooking oil in large frying pan on medium. Add cumin and chilies. Heat and stir for about 1 minute until fragrant. Add next 4 ingredients. Cook for about 10 minutes, stirring occasionally, until vegetables are softened. Cool. Add to pasta mixture.

Combine next 4 ingredients in small bowl. Add to pasta mixture. Toss. Sprinkle with green onion. Makes about 8 cups (2 L).

1 cup (250 mL): 216 Calories; 4.4 g Total Fat (1.2 g Mono, 0.7 g Poly, 1.2 g Sat); 30 mg Cholesterol; 28 g Carbohydrate; 2 g Fibre; 15 g Protein; 206 mg Sodium

Pictured on page 35.

Coconut Chicken Salad

A cool and creamy Thai-inspired salad of rice noodles and peanutty-sauced chicken, blended with a citrus coconut dressing. A refreshing, light dinner for a hot day.

Boneless, skinless chicken breast halves (4 – 6 oz., 113 – 170 g, each)	3	3
Thai peanut sauce	1/2 cup	125 mL
Water	8 cups	2 L
Small rice stick noodles	8 oz.	225 g
Sesame oil (for flavour)	1 tbsp.	15 mL
Sugar snap peas, trimmed and sliced	1 1/2 cups	375 mL
Thinly sliced red pepper	1 1/2 cups	375 mL
Julienned carrot	1 cup	250 mL
Canned coconut milk	1 cup	250 mL
Lime juice	1/4 cup	60 mL
Brown sugar, packed	2 tbsp.	30 mL
Chopped fresh cilantro	2 tbsp.	30 mL
Chili paste (sambal oelek)	1 tsp.	5 mL
Salt	1 tsp.	5 mL

Combine chicken and peanut sauce in medium bowl. Turn until coated. Marinate, covered, in refrigerator for 1 hour, turning occasionally. Transfer chicken to greased baking sheet with sides. Discard peanut sauce. Bake in 425°F (220°C) oven for about 15 minutes until internal temperature reaches 170°F (77°C). Let stand until cool enough to handle. Transfer to cutting board. Slice thinly.

Pour water into large saucepan. Bring to a boil. Add noodles. Boil, uncovered, for about 5 minutes, stirring occasionally, until tender but firm. Drain. Rinse with cold water. Drain well. Transfer to large bowl.

Add sesame oil. Toss until coated. Add next 3 ingredients and chicken.

Combine remaining 6 ingredients in small bowl. Add to noodle mixture. Toss. Makes about 9 1/2 cups (2.4 L)

1 1/2 cups (375 mL): 347 Calories; 12.7 g Total Fat (0.6 g Mono, 0.3 g Poly, 7.7 g Sat); 31 mg Cholesterol; 43 g Carbohydrate; 3 g Fibre; 17 g Protein; 755 mg Sodium

Fettuccine Frittata Salad

In Italy, frittatas are often made with yesterday's pasta—we've transformed that concept into a salad! Dig into pretty green fettuccine noodles, soft bites of egg and cheesy Asiago flavour.

Water	12 cups	3 L
Salt	1 1/2 tsp.	7 mL
Spinach fettuccine, broken in half	8 oz.	225 g
Large eggs, fork-beaten	3	3
Grated Asiago cheese	1/4 cup	60 mL
Chopped fresh chives (or sliced green onion)	1 tbsp.	15 mL
Finely diced fresh hot chili pepper (see Tip, page 81)	1/2 tsp.	2 mL
Salt	1/4 tsp.	1 mL
Pepper	1/4 tsp.	1 mL
Cooking oil	2 tsp.	10 mL
Slivered red pepper	1 cup	250 mL
Chopped tomato	3/4 cup	175 mL
Sun-dried tomato dressing	1/3 cup	75 mL
Chopped fresh basil	1 tbsp.	15 mL

Combine water and salt in Dutch oven. Bring to a boil. Add pasta. Boil, uncovered, for 11 to 13 minutes, stirring occasionally, until tender but firm. Drain. Rinse with cold water. Drain well. Transfer to large bowl.

Whisk next 6 ingredients in small bowl.

Heat cooking oil in large non-stick frying pan on medium. Pour egg mixture into pan. Reduce heat to medium-low. When starting to set at outside edge, tilt pan and gently lift cooked egg mixture with spatula, easing around pan from outside edge in. Allow uncooked egg mixture to flow onto bottom of pan until egg is softly set. Cook, covered, for about 1 minute until top is set. Transfer to cutting board. Cool. Slice into thin ribbons.

Add remaining 4 ingredients to pasta. Toss. Add egg ribbons. Toss gently. Makes about 5 3/4 cups (1.45 L).

1 cup (250 mL): 247 Calories; 9.1 g Total Fat (2.1 g Mono, 1.4 g Poly, 2.2 g Sat); 115 mg Cholesterol; 32 g Carbohydrate; 3 g Fibre; 10 g Protein; 357 mg Sodium

Chipotle Pasta Salad

Packs a spicy punch you'd never expect in a pasta salad! Smoky chipotle dressing makes for creamy pasta and chicken, accented with fresh, crunchy veggies.

Water	12 cups	3 L
Salt	1 1/2 tsp.	7 mL
Medium shell pasta	4 cups	1 L
Chopped cooked chicken (see Tip, page 41)	2 cups	500 mL
Diced celery	1 cup	250 mL
Diced red pepper	1 cup	250 mL
Diced yellow pepper	1 cup	250 mL
Sliced green onion	1/2 cup	125 mL
Sour cream	3/4 cup	175 mL
Finely chopped chipotle peppers in adobo sauce (see Tip, page 147)	1 tbsp.	15 mL
Granulated sugar	1 tbsp.	15 mL
Lime juice	1 tbsp.	15 mL
Chili powder	1 tsp.	5 mL
Dried oregano	1/2 tsp.	2 mL
Salt	1/2 tsp.	2 mL
Ground cumin	1/4 tsp.	1 mL

Combine water and salt in Dutch oven. Bring to a boil. Add pasta. Boil, uncovered, for 8 to 10 minutes, stirring occasionally, until tender but firm. Drain. Rinse with cold water. Drain well. Transfer to extra-large bowl.

Add next 5 ingredients. Toss.

Combine remaining 8 ingredients in small bowl. Add to pasta mixture. Toss. Makes about 10 cups (2.5 L).

1 1/2 cups (375 mL): 349 Calories; 8.7 g Total Fat (1.1 g Mono, 0.8 g Poly, 4.0 g Sat); 55 mg Cholesterol; 45 g Carbohydrate; 3 g Fibre; 20 g Protein; 243 mg Sodium

 tip Hot peppers contain capsaicin in the seeds and ribs. Removing the seeds and ribs will reduce the heat. Wear rubber gloves when handling hot peppers and avoid touching your eyes. Wash your hands well afterwards.

Marinated Tortellini Salad

Add protein to a marinated vegetable salad with cheese-filled pasta and flavourful havarti—a summery, filling meal salad ideal for a picnic. In a rush? Thaw frozen California mixed vegetables under hot water to replace the fresh veggies.

White vinegar	6 tbsp.	100 mL
Olive (or cooking) oil	1/4 cup	60 mL
Granulated sugar	2 tsp.	10 mL
Italian seasoning	2 tsp.	10 mL
Dry mustard	1/4 tsp.	1 mL
Garlic clove, minced	1	1
(or 1/4 tsp., 1 mL, powder)		
Salt	1/4 tsp.	1 mL
Pepper	1/4 tsp.	1 mL
Diced havarti (or mozzarella) cheese	1 1/2 cups	375 mL
Small broccoli florets	1 cup	250 mL
Small cauliflower florets	1 cup	250 mL
Chopped red pepper	1/2 cup	125 mL
Sliced red onion	1/2 cup	125 mL
Thinly sliced carrot	1/2 cup	125 mL
Water	12 cups	3 L
Salt	1 1/2 tsp.	7 mL
Package of fresh cheese tortellini	12 1/2 oz.	350 g

Whisk first 8 ingredients in large bowl.

Add next 6 ingredients. Toss. Marinate, covered, in refrigerator for 1 1/2 hours, stirring occasionally.

Combine water and salt in Dutch oven. Bring to a boil. Add pasta. Boil, uncovered, for 8 to 11 minutes, stirring occasionally, until pasta is tender but firm. Drain. Rinse with cold water. Drain well. Add to vegetable mixture. Toss. Makes about 7 cups (1.75 L).

1 cup (250 mL): 290 Calories; 13.0 g Total Fat (5.7 g Mono, 1.2 g Poly, 2.8 g Sat); 14 mg Cholesterol; 32 g Carbohydrate; 2 g Fibre; 13 g Protein; 301 mg Sodium

Veracruz Fish Salad

This light salad is inspired by a dish hailing from Veracruz, Mexico, and features authentic flavours such as olives, cilantro, chili peppers and lime.

Water	2 cups	500 mL
Long-grain white rice	1 cup	250 mL
Water	1 cup	250 mL
Lime juice	2 tbsp.	30 mL
Salt	1/2 tsp.	2 mL
Garlic clove, minced	1	1
(or 1/4 tsp., 1 mL, powder)		
Haddock fillets, any small bones removed	1 lb.	454 g
Chopped tomato	1 cup	250 mL
Sliced green olives	3/4 cup	175 mL
Finely chopped onion	1/4 cup	60 mL
Chopped fresh cilantro	2 tbsp.	30 mL
Lime juice	2 tbsp.	30 mL
Olive (or cooking) oil	1 tbsp.	15 mL
Finely diced fresh hot chili pepper	1 1/2 tsp.	7 mL
(see Tip, page 81)		
Salt	1/2 tsp.	2 mL
Pepper	1/2 tsp.	2 mL

Pour water into medium saucepan. Bring to a boil. Add rice. Stir. Reduce heat to medium-low. Simmer, covered, for 15 minutes, without stirring. Remove from heat. Let stand, covered, for about 5 minutes until rice is tender and liquid is absorbed. Fluff with fork. Transfer to large bowl. Cool.

Combine next 4 ingredients in large frying pan. Bring to a boil. Reduce heat to medium. Add fillets. Cook, covered, for about 5 minutes until fish flakes easily when tested with fork. Transfer fillets with slotted spoon to large plate. Discard cooking liquid. Let stand until cool. Break into chunks.

Add remaining 9 ingredients to rice. Stir. Add fish. Toss gently. Chill, covered, for 1 to 2 hours to blend flavours. Makes about 7 cups (1.75 L).

1 cup (250 mL): 202 Calories; 4.1 g Total Fat (2.5 g Mono, 1.0 g Poly, 0.4 g Sat); 37 mg Cholesterol; 26 g Carbohydrate; 1 g Fibre; 15 g Protein; 471 mg Sodium

Blueberry Quinoa Salad

This tasty and colourful mix of quinoa and pine nuts is tossed with fragrant garlic and herb dressing—the unique addition of dried blueberries stands out in fruity bites.

Water	1 1/2 cups	375 mL
Salt	1/8 tsp.	0.5 mL
Quinoa, rinsed and drained	2/3 cup	150 mL
Chopped arugula, lightly packed	2 cups	500 mL
Canned lentils, rinsed and drained	1 cup	250 mL
Diced red pepper	1/2 cup	125 mL
Dried blueberries	1/2 cup	125 mL
Grated Swiss cheese	1/4 cup	60 mL
Pine nuts, toasted (see Tip, page 134)	1/4 cup	60 mL
Thinly sliced green onion	2 tbsp.	30 mL
Olive (or cooking) oil	3 tbsp.	50 mL
Raspberry vinegar	3 tbsp.	50 mL
Lemon juice	1 1/2 tsp.	7 mL
Granulated sugar	3/4 tsp.	4 mL
Salt	3/4 tsp.	4 mL
Pepper	3/4 tsp.	4 mL
Garlic clove, minced	1	1
(or 1/4 tsp., 1 mL, powder)		

Combine water and salt in small saucepan. Bring to a boil. Add quinoa. Stir. Reduce heat to medium-low. Simmer, covered, for about 20 minutes, without stirring, until quinoa is tender and liquid is absorbed. Transfer to large bowl. Cool.

Add next 7 ingredients.

Whisk remaining 7 ingredients in small bowl. Add to quinoa mixture. Toss. Makes about 6 cups (1.5 L).

1 cup (250 mL): 275 Calories; 13.6 g Total Fat (6.4 g Mono, 3.4 g Poly, 2.2 g Sat); 6 mg Cholesterol; 30 g Carbohydrate; 7 g Fibre; 8 g Protein; 409 mg Sodium

Pictured on page 89.

Peachy Chickpea Salad

A complementary match—the appealing sweetness of peaches paired with a chili dressing. Chickpeas and a variety of fresh veggies make this a filling salad.

Can of chickpeas (garbanzo beans), rinsed and drained	19 oz.	540 mL
Can of sliced peaches in syrup, drained and syrup reserved, chopped	14 oz.	398 mL
Diced peeled jicama	1 cup	250 mL
Chopped green pepper	1/2 cup	125 mL
Chopped red pepper	1/2 cup	125 mL
Sliced green onion	1/4 cup	60 mL
CHILI DRESSING		
Chopped fresh cilantro (or parsley)	2 tbsp.	30 mL
Olive (or cooking) oil	2 tbsp.	30 mL
Red wine vinegar	2 tbsp.	30 mL
Reserved peach syrup	2 tbsp.	30 mL
Chili powder	1 tbsp.	15 mL
Dried oregano	1/2 tsp.	2 mL
Salt	1/2 tsp.	2 mL
Garlic clove, minced (or 1/4 tsp., 1 mL, powder)	1	1
Cayenne pepper	1/8 tsp.	0.5 mL

Toss first 6 ingredients in large bowl.

Chili Dressing: Whisk all 9 ingredients in small bowl. Add to chickpea mixture. Toss. Chill for 30 minutes to blend flavours. Makes about 6 cups (1.5 L).

1 cup (250 mL): 186 Calories; 6.2 g Total Fat (3.7 g Mono, 1.4 g Poly, 0.7 g Sat); 0 mg Cholesterol; 30 g Carbohydrate; 7 g Fibre; 5 g Protein; 297 mg Sodium

Edamame Salad

Edamame is the Japanese word for fresh soybeans, and soy means good for you! This appetizing blend of smooth green edamame and sliced radishes is coated with a zesty ginger and sesame dressing.

Water	6 cups	1.5 L
Salt	1/2 tsp.	2 mL
Frozen shelled edamame (soybeans)	3 cups	750 mL
Chopped fresh spinach leaves, lightly packed	3 cups	750 mL
Chopped English cucumber (with peel), 1/2 inch (12 mm) pieces	1 cup	250 mL
Chopped red pepper (1/2 inch, 12 mm, pieces)	1 cup	250 mL
Sliced radish	1 cup	250 mL
Mayonnaise	3 tbsp.	50 mL
Rice vinegar	2 tbsp.	30 mL
Liquid honey	1 tbsp.	15 mL
Sesame oil (for flavour)	1 tbsp.	15 mL
Soy sauce	1 tbsp.	15 mL
Finely grated ginger root	1 tsp.	5 mL
Salt	1/2 tsp.	2 mL
Pepper	1/4 tsp.	1 mL

Combine water and salt in large saucepan. Bring to a boil. Add edamame. Reduce heat to medium. Boil gently, uncovered, for 5 minutes. Drain. Rinse with cold water. Drain well. Transfer to large bowl.

Add next 4 ingredients.

Whisk remaining 8 ingredients in small bowl. Add to spinach mixture. Toss. Makes about 8 1/2 cups (2.1 L).

1 cup (250 mL): 141 Calories; 7.8 g Total Fat (trace Mono, 0.1 g Poly, 0.8 g Sat); 2 mg Cholesterol; 11 g Carbohydrate; 4 g Fibre; 6 g Protein; 354 mg Sodium

Pictured on page 89.

Wrapped-Up Fiesta Tuna

Fresh crunchy jicama and Mexican spices add a little fiesta to ordinary tuna salad. Wrap in plastic wrap to take for lunch the next day—these will keep well in the refrigerator for up to two days.

Can of red kidney beans, rinsed and drained	14 oz.	398 mL
Chopped peeled jicama	1 cup	250 mL
Can of chunk light tuna in water, drained	6 oz.	170 g
Salsa	1/3 cup	75 mL
Mayonnaise	1/4 cup	60 mL
Slivered red pepper	1/4 cup	60 mL
Chopped fresh cilantro (or parsley)	2 tbsp.	30 mL
Lime juice	2 tsp.	10 mL
Chili powder	1/4 tsp.	1 mL
Salt	1/4 tsp.	1 mL
Shredded romaine lettuce, lightly packed	1 cup	250 mL
Whole-wheat flour tortillas (9 inch, 22 cm, diameter)	4	4

Combine first 10 ingredients in large bowl.

Arrange 1/4 cup (60 mL) lettuce across centre of each tortilla. Spoon 1 cup (250 mL) tuna mixture over lettuce. Fold sides over filling. Roll up from bottom to enclose filling. Makes 4 salad wraps.

1 salad wrap: 368 Calories; 13.3 g Total Fat (0.4 g Mono, 0.7 g Poly, 1.9 g Sat); 23 mg Cholesterol; 46 g Carbohydrate; 13 g Fibre; 21 g Protein; 627 mg Sodium

Paré Pointer

If you can't swim, do you have to wear a lifejacket to sleep on a waterbed?

Satay Chicken Salad Wraps

Combined with rice paper rolls, tangy-sweet Thai-flavoured chicken salad becomes finger food! Wrap well in plastic wrap and enjoy these cold salad rolls for lunch at work. A great way to use leftover rice.

Peanut sauce	2 tbsp.	30 mL
Lime juice	1 tsp.	5 mL
Liquid honey	1 tsp.	5 mL
Ground coriander	1/4 tsp.	1 mL
Cooked long-grain white rice	1/2 cup	125 mL
Chopped cooked chicken	1/3 cup	75 mL
(see Tip, page 41)		
Grated carrot	2 tbsp.	30 mL
Grated English cucumber (with peel)	2 tbsp.	30 mL
Finely chopped green onion	2 tsp.	10 mL
Rice paper rounds	2	2
(9 inch, 22 cm, diameter)		

Whisk first 4 ingredients in small bowl.

Add next 5 ingredients. Stir.

Place 1 rice paper round in shallow bowl of hot water until just softened. Place on work surface. Spoon about 2/3 cup (150 mL) chicken mixture in centre. Fold sides over filling. Roll up tightly from bottom to enclose filling. Repeat with remaining rice paper round and chicken mixture. Makes 2 salad wraps.

1 salad wrap: 188 Calories; 5.9 g Total Fat (2.5 g Mono, 1.5 g Poly, 1.4 g Sat); 21 mg Cholesterol; 23 g Carbohydrate; 1 g Fibre; 10 g Protein; 173 mg Sodium

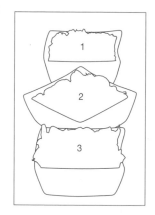

1. Blueberry Quinoa Salad, page 84
2. Edamame Salad, page 86
3. California Roll Salad, page 112

Props: Cherison

Greek Chicken Bean Salad

Easy to prepare and satisfying to eat, this hearty bean, veggie and feta blend has mild Greek flavours highlighted by a simple, tzatziki-based dressing.

Tzatziki	3/4 cup	175 mL
Lemon juice	1 tbsp.	15 mL
Dried oregano	1 1/2 tsp.	7 mL
Salt	1/4 tsp.	1 mL
Cans of mixed beans (19 oz., 540 mL, each), rinsed and drained	2	2
Chopped cooked chicken (see Tip, page 141)	2 cups	500 mL
Diced green pepper	1 1/2 cups	375 mL
Cherry tomatoes, halved	1 cup	250 mL
Diced English cucumber (with peel)	1 cup	250 mL
Kalamata olives, pitted and chopped	3/4 cup	175 mL
Crumbled feta cheese	1/4 cup	60 mL

Combine first 4 ingredients in large bowl.

Add remaining 7 ingredients. Stir well. Makes about 9 cups (2.25 L).

1 cup (250 mL): 196 Calories; 5.8 g Total Fat (1.9 g Mono, 0.7 g Poly, 2.1 g Sat); 31 mg Cholesterol; 21 g Carbohydrate; 6 g Fibre; 17 g Protein; 375 mg Sodium

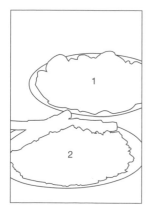

1. Summer Spinach Salad, page 27
2. Antipasto Wheat Salad, page 104

West Coast Salmon Salad

Enjoy the appealing flavours and colours of the Canadian west coast. Wild rice is paired with rich salmon and tart apples, all tossed in sweet and fruity vinaigrette.

Prepared chicken broth	2 1/2 cups	625 mL
Salt	1/4 tsp.	1 mL
Wild rice	1 cup	250 mL
Raspberry vinaigrette dressing	2/3 cup	150 mL
Maple syrup	2 tbsp.	30 mL
Salt	1/8 tsp.	0.5 mL
Pepper, just a pinch		
Salmon fillets, skin-on, any small bones removed	1 lb.	454 g
Spring mix lettuce, lightly packed	2 cups	500 mL
Chopped unpeeled tart apple (such as Granny Smith)	1 1/2 cups	375 mL
Chopped fresh chives	2 tbsp.	30 mL

Combine broth and salt in medium saucepan. Bring to a boil. Add rice. Stir. Reduce heat to medium-low. Simmer, covered, for about 60 minutes, without stirring, until rice is tender. Drain any remaining liquid. Transfer to large bowl. Let stand until cool.

Add dressing. Stir. Chill, covered, for 1 hour.

Combine next 3 ingredients in small bowl. Brush over fillets. Preheat gas barbecue to medium (see Tip, page 50). Cook fillets on greased grill for about 4 minutes per side until fish flakes easily when tested with fork. Let stand until cool enough to handle. Remove and discard skin. Break fillets into large chunks.

Add remaining 3 ingredients and salmon to rice mixture. Toss gently. Makes about 7 1/2 cups (1.9 L).

1 cup (250 mL): 287 Calories; 12.7 g Total Fat (2.9 g Mono, 2.0 g Poly, 2.0 g Sat); 30 mg Cholesterol; 28 g Carbohydrate; 2 g Fibre; 16 g Protein; 807 mg Sodium

Pictured on front cover.

Asian Chicken Salad

This chicken and rice salad, loaded with crunchy vegetables, can be made the day before. Simply chill it until you need it—perfect for potlucks.

Water	1 1/3 cups	325 mL
Long-grain white rice	2/3 cup	150 mL
Prepared chicken broth	1 cup	250 mL
Soy sauce	2 tsp.	10 mL
Ground ginger	1/4 tsp.	1 mL
Boneless, skinless chicken breast halves	1 lb.	454 g
Can of bamboo shoots, drained	8 oz.	227 mL
Asian-style sesame dressing	1/2 cup	125 mL
Thinly sliced celery	1/2 cup	125 mL
Chopped red pepper	1/4 cup	60 mL
Sliced green onion	1/4 cup	60 mL
Slivered almonds, toasted (see Tip, page 134)	3 tbsp.	50 mL
Soy sauce	1 tbsp.	15 mL
Can of mandarin orange segments, drained	10 oz.	284 mL

Pour water into medium saucepan. Bring to a boil. Add rice. Stir. Reduce heat to medium-low. Simmer, covered, for about 15 minutes, without stirring, until rice is tender and liquid is absorbed. Fluff with fork. Transfer to large bowl.

Combine next 3 ingredients in large frying pan. Bring to a boil. Reduce heat to medium-low. Add chicken. Simmer, covered, for about 15 minutes until internal temperature of chicken reaches 170°F (77°C). Drain (see Note). Transfer to cutting board. Let stand until cool enough to handle. Cut into 3/4 inch (2 cm) pieces. Add to rice. Stir.

Add next 7 ingredients and 1/3 cup (75 mL) orange segments. Toss gently. Scatter remaining orange segments over top. Chill, covered, for 1 hour to blend flavours. Makes about 7 cups (1.75 L).

1 cup (250 mL): 310 Calories; 6.7 g Total Fat (1.3 g Mono, 0.7 g Poly, 1.0 g Sat); 38 mg Cholesterol; 42 g Carbohydrate; 2 g Fibre; 20 g Protein; 756 mg Sodium

Note: Save the leftover chicken broth for another use. It makes an excellent broth for a bowl of Asian-flavoured chicken soup.

Two-Bean Pita Salad

Enjoy this fresh, Lebanese-inspired blend. The pleasing textures of chickpeas and kidney beans are a nice complement to crunchy vegetables and baked pita chips. Garnish with additional parsley and mint if desired.

Whole-wheat pita bread (7 inch, 18 cm, diameter)	1	1
Olive oil	1 tsp.	5 mL
Sesame seeds, toasted (see Tip, page 134)	1/4 tsp.	1 mL
Dried thyme	1/8 tsp.	0.5 mL
Salt, sprinkle		
Can of chickpeas (garbanzo beans), rinsed and drained	19 oz.	540 mL
Can of white kidney beans, rinsed and drained	19 oz.	540 mL
Chopped fresh parsley (or 2 1/4 tsp., 11 mL, dried)	3 tbsp.	50 mL
Lemon juice	2 tbsp.	30 mL
Olive oil	2 tbsp.	30 mL
Chopped fresh mint (or 3/4 tsp., 4 mL, dried)	1 tbsp.	15 mL
Ground allspice	1/4 tsp.	1 mL
Salt	1/4 tsp.	1 mL
Pepper	1/8 tsp.	0.5 mL
Shredded romaine lettuce, lightly packed	2 cups	500 mL
Large tomatoes, cut into wedges	2	2
Sliced English cucumber (with peel)	1 cup	250 mL
Thinly sliced red onion	1/4 cup	60 mL

Brush both sides of pita with olive oil. Sprinkle with next 3 ingredients. Arrange on ungreased baking sheet with sides. Bake in 325°F (160°C) oven for about 10 minutes per side until crisp and dry. Transfer to wire rack to cool. Break into 1 inch (2.5 cm) pieces.

Combine next 9 ingredients in large bowl.

Add remaining 4 ingredients. Toss. Sprinkle with pita. Makes about 8 cups (2 L).

1 cup (250 mL): 183 Calories; 6.1 g Total Fat (3.2 g Mono, 1.3 g Poly, 0.7 g Sat); 0 mg Cholesterol; 26 g Carbohydrate; 7 g Fibre; 8 g Protein; 213 mg Sodium

Jamaican Chicken Salad

An eye-catching salad, this mildly spicy blend offers the Caribbean-inspired combination of rice and beans paired with the sweetness of mango.

Can of coconut milk	14 oz.	398 mL
Water	1/4 cup	60 mL
Salt	1/2 tsp.	2 mL
Ground nutmeg, just a pinch		
White basmati rice	1 cup	250 mL
Boneless, skinless chicken thighs, halved	1 lb.	454 g
Jerk seasoning paste	2 tsp.	10 mL
Can of red kidney beans, rinsed and drained	19 oz.	540 mL
Shredded romaine lettuce, lightly packed	1 1/2 cups	375 mL
Diced frozen mango pieces, thawed	1 cup	250 mL
Finely chopped green onion	1/4 cup	60 mL
Lime juice	3 tbsp.	50 mL
Olive (or cooking) oil	2 tbsp.	30 mL
Granulated sugar	1 tsp.	5 mL
Dried thyme	1/4 tsp.	1 mL
Salt	1/4 tsp.	1 mL

Combine first 4 ingredients in medium saucepan. Bring to a boil. Add rice. Stir. Reduce heat to medium-low. Simmer, covered, for 15 minutes, without stirring. Remove from heat. Let stand, covered, for about 5 minutes until rice is tender and liquid is absorbed. Fluff with fork. Transfer to large bowl. Let stand until cool.

Place chicken in medium bowl. Add seasoning paste. Stir until coated. Arrange on greased baking sheet with sides. Bake in 375°F (190°C) oven for about 15 minutes per side until internal temperature reaches 170°F (77°C). Transfer to cutting board. Let stand until cool enough to handle. Chop. Add to rice.

Add next 4 ingredients.

Whisk remaining 5 ingredients in small bowl. Add to rice mixture. Toss. Makes about 9 cups (2.25 L).

1 cup (250 mL): 310 Calories; 16.7 g Total Fat (4.1 g Mono, 1.4 g Poly, 9.9 g Sat); 33 mg Cholesterol; 27 g Carbohydrate; 6 g Fibre; 15 g Protein; 294 mg Sodium

Moroccan Wild Rice Salad

An intriguing look with lots of wild rice and almond texture, with soft bites of chicken and sweet potato. This dish is exotic, yet has a rustic feel, making it ideal for an autumn dinner.

Water	2 1/2 cups	625 mL
Salt	1/4 tsp.	1 mL
Wild rice	1 cup	250 mL
Canned sweet potato, drained	1 cup	250 mL
Chopped cooked chicken (see Tip, page 41)	1 cup	250 mL
Golden raisins	1/2 cup	125 mL
Slivered almonds, toasted (see Tip, page 134)	1/2 cup	125 mL
Chopped fresh parsley (or 1 1/2 tsp., 7 mL, dried)	2 tbsp.	30 mL
MOROCCAN VINAIGRETTE		
Ground coriander	1/2 tsp.	2 mL
Ground cumin	1/2 tsp.	2 mL
Ground cinnamon	1/4 tsp.	1 mL
Ground ginger	1/4 tsp.	1 mL
Cayenne pepper	1/8 tsp.	0.5 mL
Apple cider vinegar	1/4 cup	60 mL
Olive (or cooking) oil	1/4 cup	60 mL
Orange juice	1/4 cup	60 mL
Granulated sugar	1/2 tsp.	2 mL
Grated orange zest	1/4 tsp.	1 mL
Salt	1/4 tsp.	1 mL

Combine water and salt in medium saucepan. Bring to a boil. Add rice. Stir. Reduce heat to medium-low. Simmer, covered, for about 60 minutes, without stirring, until rice is tender. Drain any remaining liquid. Transfer to large bowl. Cool.

Add next 5 ingredients.

Moroccan Vinaigrette: Heat small frying pan on medium. Add first 5 ingredients. Heat and stir for about 1 minute until fragrant. Transfer to small bowl.

(continued on next page)

Add remaining 6 ingredients. Whisk. Makes about 7/8 cup (200 mL). Add to rice mixture. Toss. Makes about 5 cups (1.25 L).

1 cup (250 mL): 454 Calories; 19.4 g Total Fat (12.3 g Mono, 3.7 g Poly, 2.7 g Sat); 25 mg Cholesterol; 56 g Carbohydrate; 6 g Fibre; 17 g Protein; 307 mg Sodium

Pictured on page 108.

Russian Wild Rice Salad

Good, simple flavours come together in this salad made creamy with Russian-style dressing. Sweet pickled beets and roast beef strips are paired with the earthier flavours of wild rice and spinach.

Water	1 1/2 cups	375 mL
Salt	1/8 tsp.	0.5 mL
Wild rice	1/2 cup	125 mL
Sour cream	1/3 cup	75 mL
Chopped fresh dill (or 3/4 tsp., 4 mL, dried)	1 tbsp.	15 mL
White wine vinegar	1 tbsp.	15 mL
Dry mustard	1 tsp.	5 mL
Coarsely ground pepper	1/2 tsp.	2 mL
Granulated sugar	1/2 tsp.	2 mL
Hot pepper sauce	1/8 tsp.	0.5 mL
Chopped fresh spinach leaves, lightly packed	2 cups	500 mL
Deli roast beef slices, cut into thin strips	6 oz.	170 g
Diced pickled beets	2/3 cup	150 mL
Diced English cucumber (with peel)	1/2 cup	125 mL
Finely diced pickled onions	1 tbsp.	15 mL

Combine water and salt in small saucepan. Bring to a boil. Add rice. Stir. Reduce heat to medium-low. Simmer, covered, for about 60 minutes, without stirring, until rice is tender. Drain any remaining liquid. Cool.

Whisk next 7 ingredients in large bowl.

Add remaining 5 ingredients and rice. Toss. Makes about 6 cups (1.5 L).

1 cup (250 mL): 131 Calories; 3.5 g Total Fat (0.1 g Mono, 0.2 g Poly, 1.9 g Sat); 25 mg Cholesterol; 16 g Carbohydrate; 2 g Fibre; 9 g Protein; 286 mg Sodium

Pictured on page 107 and on back cover.

Curried Quinoa Salad

This pilaf-like salad features nutritious quinoa (KEEN-wah) paired with the lovely flavours of tangy curry and lemon. The addition of chicken and beans makes for a protein-packed meal.

Water	1 cup	250 mL
Salt	1/4 tsp.	1 mL
Quinoa, rinsed and drained	2/3 cup	150 mL
Can of mixed beans, rinsed and drained	19 oz.	540 mL
Chopped cooked chicken (see Tip, page 41)	1 cup	250 mL
Chopped celery	3/4 cup	175 mL
Thinly sliced red onion	1/2 cup	125 mL
Lemon juice	3 tbsp.	50 mL
Olive (or cooking) oil	3 tbsp.	50 mL
Curry powder	1 1/2 tsp.	7 mL
Finely grated ginger root	1 tsp.	5 mL
Salt	1/2 tsp.	2 mL
Garlic clove, minced (or 1/4 tsp., 1 mL, powder)	1	1
Chopped fresh cilantro (or parsley), optional	1 tbsp.	15 mL

Combine water and salt in medium saucepan. Bring to a boil. Add quinoa. Stir. Reduce heat to medium-low. Simmer, covered, for about 20 minutes, without stirring, until quinoa is tender and liquid is absorbed. Transfer to large bowl. Cool.

Add next 4 ingredients.

Whisk next 6 ingredients in small bowl. Add to quinoa mixture. Stir.

Sprinkle with cilantro. Makes about 5 cups (1.25 L).

1 cup (250 mL): 307 Calories; 12.3 g Total Fat (7.1 g Mono, 2.2 g Poly, 1.9 g Sat); 25 mg Cholesterol; 35 g Carbohydrate; 6 g Fibre; 17 g Protein; 517 mg Sodium

Paré Pointer

Who cornered the spice market? Some guy named Herb.

Beef Bulgur Salad

This pretty, confetti-like bulgur salad is sprinkled with bright bits of vegetables and mint, with tender sirloin to boost the protein.

Water	1 1/2 cups	375 mL
Bulgur	1 cup	250 mL
Olive oil	3 tbsp.	50 mL
Lemon juice	2 tbsp.	30 mL
Liquid honey	1 tbsp.	15 mL
Grated lemon zest	1/2 tsp.	2 mL
Salt	1/2 tsp.	2 mL
Pepper	1/4 tsp.	1 mL
Finely chopped red pepper	1 cup	250 mL
Finely chopped yellow pepper	1 cup	250 mL
Finely chopped English cucumber (with peel)	1/2 cup	125 mL
Finely chopped red onion	1/2 cup	125 mL
Chopped fresh mint (or 3/4 tsp., 4 mL, dried)	1 tbsp.	15 mL
Cooking oil	1 tsp.	5 mL
Beef top sirloin steak, diced	3/4 lb.	340 g
Ground cumin	1 tsp.	5 mL
Garlic cloves, minced (or 1/2 tsp., 2 mL, powder)	2	2
Salt	1/4 tsp.	1 mL

Pour water into small saucepan. Bring to a boil. Add bulgur. Stir. Remove from heat. Let stand, covered, for about 30 minutes until bulgur is tender and liquid is absorbed. Fluff with fork. Transfer to large bowl.

Whisk next 6 ingredients in small bowl. Add to bulgur.

Add next 5 ingredients. Stir.

Heat cooking oil in large frying pan on medium-high. Add remaining 4 ingredients. Cook for about 2 minutes, stirring often, until beef is browned. Add to bulgur mixture. Stir. Makes about 6 cups (1.5 L).

1 cup (250 mL): 270 Calories; 12.3 g Total Fat (7.1 g Mono, 1.6 g Poly, 2.7 g Sat); 30 mg Cholesterol; 26 g Carbohydrate; 5 g Fibre; 16 g Protein; 322 mg Sodium

Persian Rice Salad

Vibrant rice, bites of veggies and well-seasoned lamb meatballs—a tasty and colourful combination. Allspice and turmeric lend an exotic air.

Water	2 cups	500 mL
Turmeric	1/4 tsp.	1 mL
Salt	1/8 tsp.	0.5 mL
White basmati rice	1 cup	250 mL
Chopped English cucumber (with peel)	1 cup	250 mL
Chopped tomato	1 cup	250 mL
Frozen tiny peas, thawed	1 cup	250 mL
Grated carrot	1 cup	250 mL
Chopped fresh chives	2 tbsp.	30 mL
(or 1 1/2 tsp., 7 mL, dried)		

PERSIAN MEATBALLS

Large egg, fork-beaten	1	1
Fine dry bread crumbs	1/2 cup	125 mL
Finely chopped onion	2 tbsp.	30 mL
Ground allspice	3/4 tsp.	4 mL
Salt	1/2 tsp.	2 mL
Pepper	1/8 tsp.	0.5 mL
Lean ground lamb (or beef)	1 lb.	454 g

ORANGE HONEY DRESSING

Liquid honey	2 tbsp.	30 mL
Olive (or cooking) oil	2 tbsp.	30 mL
Orange juice	2 tbsp.	30 mL
Red wine vinegar	2 tbsp.	30 mL
Grated orange zest	1 1/2 tsp.	7 mL
Salt	1/4 tsp.	1 mL

Combine first 3 ingredients in medium saucepan. Bring to a boil. Add rice. Stir. Reduce heat to medium-low. Simmer, covered, for 15 minutes, without stirring. Remove from heat. Let stand, covered, for about 5 minutes until rice is tender and liquid is absorbed. Fluff with fork. Transfer to extra-large bowl. Cool.

Add next 5 ingredients. Toss. Chill, covered.

(continued on next page)

Persian Meatballs: Combine first 6 ingredients in large bowl.

Add lamb. Mix well. Roll into balls using 1 tbsp. (15 mL) for each. Arrange in single layer on greased baking sheet with sides. Bake in 450°F (230°C) oven for about 12 minutes until no longer pink inside. Makes about 35 meatballs.

Orange Honey Dressing: Whisk all 6 ingredients in small bowl. Makes about 1/2 cup (125 mL). Add Persian Meatballs and Orange Honey Dressing to rice mixture. Toss. Makes about 10 cups (2.5 L).

1 1/2 cups (375 mL): 350 Calories; 12.7 g Total Fat (3.0 g Mono, 0.7 g Poly, 3.7 g Sat); 76 mg Cholesterol; 39 g Carbohydrate; 4 g Fibre; 20 g Protein; 471 mg Sodium

Pictured on page 107 and on back cover.

Black Bean Salad Boats

Crisp romaine leaves are filled with creamy bean, corn and chicken salad. The fun-to-eat, crunchy "boats" make for family-friendly fare.

Hot salsa	1/2 cup	125 mL
Mayonnaise	1/4 cup	60 mL
Chili powder	1/4 tsp.	1 mL
Garlic clove, minced	1	1
(or 1/4 tsp., 1 mL, powder)		
Ground cumin	1/4 tsp.	1 mL
Can of black beans, rinsed and drained	19 oz.	540 mL
Can of kernel corn, drained	12 oz.	341 mL
Chopped cooked chicken (see Tip, page 41)	1 cup	250 mL
Diced orange pepper	1/2 cup	125 mL
Sliced green onion	1/4 cup	60 mL
Romaine lettuce heart leaves	16	16

Combine first 5 ingredients in small bowl.

Add next 5 ingredients. Stir to coat. Chill, covered, for 1 hour to blend flavours.

Spoon 1/4 cup (60 mL) black bean mixture into each lettuce leaf. Makes 16 salad boats.

1 salad boat: 94 Calories; 3.7 g Total Fat (0.2 g Mono, 0.4 g Poly, 0.6 g Sat); 9 mg Cholesterol; 10 g Carbohydrate; 3 g Fibre; 5 g Protein; 237 mg Sodium

Variation: Instead of salad boats, chop romaine lettuce and toss with black bean mixture.

Legumes & Grains

Lamb Bulgur Salad

Lamb chops spiced with the warm flavours of cinnamon, cumin and ginger rest atop a bed of fresh vegetable bulgar salad. Prepare the bulgur while the rack of lamb is in the oven.

Boiling water	3/4 cup	175 mL
Bulgur, fine grind	1/3 cup	75 mL
Balkan-style yogurt	1 tbsp.	15 mL
Ground almonds	1 tbsp.	15 mL
Liquid honey	2 tsp.	10 mL
Ground cinnamon	1/2 tsp.	2 mL
Ground cumin	1/2 tsp.	2 mL
Ground ginger	1/2 tsp.	2 mL
Garlic clove, minced	1	1
(or 1/4 tsp., 1 mL, powder)		
Salt	1/4 tsp.	1 mL
Rack of lamb (about 1 lb., 454 g)	1	1
Olive (or cooking) oil	1/4 cup	60 mL
Lemon juice	2 tbsp.	30 mL
Salt	1 tsp.	5 mL
Finely chopped fresh parsley	1 cup	250 mL
Finely chopped zucchini (with peel)	1 cup	250 mL
Finely chopped carrot	1/2 cup	125 mL
Finely chopped red pepper	1/2 cup	125 mL
Finely chopped green onion	2 tbsp.	30 mL
Small garlic clove, minced	1	1
(or 1/8 tsp., 0.5 mL, powder)		

Combine boiling water and bulgur in small heatproof bowl. Stir. Let stand, covered, for about 20 minutes until bulgur is tender. Drain well.

Combine next 8 ingredients in small cup. Spread over lamb. Place, meat-side up, on greased baking sheet with sides. Cook in 400°F (205°C) oven for about 30 minutes until internal temperature reaches 145°F (63°C) for medium-rare or until lamb reaches desired doneness. Transfer to cutting board. Cover with foil. Let stand for 10 minutes. Cut into 1-bone portions.

Whisk next 3 ingredients in medium bowl.

(continued on next page)

Add remaining 6 ingredients and bulgur. Stir. Transfer to 4 serving plates. Arrange lamb over bulgur mixture. Serves 4.

1 serving: 392 Calories; 24.6 g Total Fat (14.2 g Mono, 2.7 g Poly, 6.1 g Sat); 75 mg Cholesterol; 18 g Carbohydrate; 4 g Fibre; 26 g Protein; 847 mg Sodium

Beef and Barley Salad

This comforting combination makes a hearty and satisfying meal, and is a great way to use leftover grilled steak or roast beef. Try garnishing with leafy celery stalks for a beautiful finishing touch.

Prepared beef broth	2 1/3 cups	575 mL
Pot barley	2/3 cup	150 mL
Chopped cooked roast beef	1 1/2 cups	375 mL
Cherry tomatoes, quartered	1 cup	250 mL
Chopped celery	1 cup	250 mL
Chopped pickled onions	1/2 cup	125 mL
Red wine vinegar	1/4 cup	60 mL
Cooking oil	2 tbsp.	30 mL
Chopped fresh thyme	2 tsp.	10 mL
(or 1/2 tsp., 2 mL, dried)		
Salt	1/4 tsp.	1 mL
Pepper, just a pinch		
Shredded fresh spinach leaves,	2 cups	500 mL
lightly packed		
Bacon slices, cooked crisp and crumbled	4	4
Chopped fresh parsley	1 tsp.	5 mL
(or 1/4 tsp., 1 mL, dried)		

Pour broth into small saucepan. Bring to a boil. Add barley. Stir. Reduce heat to medium-low. Simmer, covered, for about 1 hour, without stirring, until barley is tender and liquid is absorbed. Rinse with cold water. Drain well. Transfer to large bowl. Cool.

Add next 4 ingredients.

Combine next 5 ingredients in small bowl. Add to barley mixture. Stir.

Add remaining 3 ingredients. Toss. Makes about 6 1/2 cups (1.6 L).

1 cup (250 mL): 213 Calories; 9.0 g Total Fat (4.3 g Mono, 1.6 g Poly, 1.8 g Sat); 35 mg Cholesterol; 19 g Carbohydrate; 4 g Fibre; 14 g Protein; 837 mg Sodium

Antipasto Wheat Salad

Wheat berries are combined with traditional antipasto fare for this colourful meal salad. Prep everything else while the wheat is cooking.

Hard red wheat	1 cup	250 mL
Water, to cover		
Water	2 1/2 cups	625 mL
Salt	1/4 tsp.	1 mL
Sun-dried tomato dressing	1/2 cup	125 mL
Sun-dried tomatoes in oil, blotted dry and chopped	2 tbsp.	30 mL
Frozen cut green beans, thawed	1 cup	250 mL
Ice water		
Diced bocconcini (see Note)	1 1/4 cups	300 mL
Jar of marinated artichoke hearts, drained and chopped	6 oz.	170 mL
Diced seeded Roma (plum) tomatoes	1/2 cup	125 mL
Finely diced deli ham	1/2 cup	125 mL
Chopped fresh rosemary	1 tsp.	5 mL
Deli ham slices, halved lengthwise	4	4
Bread sticks	8	8

Place wheat into small bowl. Cover with first amount of water. Let stand for at least 6 hours or overnight. Drain.

Combine second amount of water and salt in small saucepan. Bring to a boil. Add wheat. Stir. Reduce heat to medium-low. Simmer, covered, for about 1 3/4 hours, without stirring, until wheat is tender. Drain any remaining liquid. Rinse under cold water. Drain well. Transfer to large bowl.

Add dressing and sun-dried tomato. Stir.

Pour water into medium saucepan until about 1 inch (2.5 cm) deep. Add green beans. Bring to a boil. Reduce heat to medium. Boil gently, covered, for about 3 minutes until bright green. Drain.

Plunge into ice water in separate large bowl. Let stand for 10 minutes until cold. Drain. Transfer to cutting board. Chop. Add to wheat mixture.

Add next 5 ingredients. Stir.

(continued on next page)

104 Legumes & Grains

Wrap half slice of ham around 1 end of each bread stick. Serve with salad. Serves 4.

1 serving: 550 Calories; 23.8 g Total Fat (1.2 g Mono, 1.2 g Poly, 6.0 g Sat); 44 mg Cholesterol; 58 g Carbohydrate; 8 g Fibre; 32 g Protein; 1413 mg Sodium

Note: Bocconcini are balls of fresh mozzarella cheese.

Pictured on page 90.

Tapenade Lentil Salad

A hearty, bistro-style salad for olive lovers! This earth-toned blend has fabulous texture from sweet, tender scallops and soft lentils.

Olive oil	1 tsp.	5 mL
Large sea scallops, halved horizontally	1 lb.	454 g
Pepper	1/2 tsp.	2 mL
Coarsely chopped large pitted green olives	1/2 cup	125 mL
Coarsely chopped pitted whole black olives	1/2 cup	125 mL
Olive oil	2 tbsp.	30 mL
Sun-dried tomatoes in oil, blotted dry, coarsely chopped	2 tbsp.	30 mL
Capers (optional)	2 tsp.	10 mL
Chopped fresh basil	1 tsp.	5 mL
Chopped fresh thyme	1 tsp.	5 mL
Small garlic clove, minced	1	1
Chopped fresh oregano	1/2 tsp.	2 mL
Anchovy paste	1/4 tsp.	1 mL
Cans of lentils (19 oz., 540 mL, each), rinsed and drained	2	2
Chopped fresh parsley	1/4 cup	60 mL

Heat large frying pan or wok on medium-high until very hot. Add first amount of olive oil. Add scallops. Sprinkle with pepper. Stir-fry for about 2 minutes until opaque. Transfer to plate. Cool.

Place next 10 ingredients in food processor. Process with on/off motion until finely chopped. Transfer to large bowl.

Add lentils, parsley and scallops. Stir. Makes about 6 1/2 cups (1.6 L).

1 cup (250 mL): 264 Calories; 8.3 g Total Fat (5.6 g Mono, 1.4 g Poly, 1.0 g Sat); 23 mg Cholesterol; 26 g Carbohydrate; 12 g Fibre; 22 g Protein; 577 mg Sodium

Beans 'n' Greens Salad

A tangy twist on traditional bean salad—roast beef and crisp lettuce are tossed in to make it a meal. Throw it together with leftover beef and enjoy for lunch!

Cans of mixed beans (19 oz., 540 mL, each), rinsed and drained	2	2
Cut or torn romaine lettuce, lightly packed	3 cups	750 mL
Diced cooked roast beef	1 cup	250 mL
Chopped red pepper	1/2 cup	125 mL
Grated carrot	1/2 cup	125 mL
ONION VINAIGRETTE		
White vinegar	1/2 cup	125 mL
Cooking oil	1/4 cup	60 mL
Finely chopped onion	1/4 cup	60 mL
Granulated sugar	2 tbsp.	30 mL
Dry mustard	1/2 tsp.	2 mL
Salt	1/2 tsp.	2 mL
Pepper	1/4 tsp.	1 mL
Paprika	1/4 tsp.	1 mL

Toss first 5 ingredients in large bowl.

Onion Vinaigrette: Whisk all 8 ingredients in small bowl. Drizzle over bean mixture. Toss. Makes about 8 cups (2 L).

1 cup (250 mL): 227 Calories; 9.2 g Total Fat (4.7 g Mono, 2.1 g Poly, 1.1 g Sat); 18 mg Cholesterol; 25 g Carbohydrate; 6 g Fibre; 14 g Protein; 326 mg Sodium

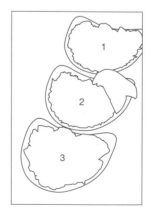

1. Persian Rice Salad, page 100
2. Russian Wild Rice Salad, page 97
3. Berry Brie Salad, page 39

Props: Hutschenreuther

Lentil Vegetable Salad

Chill out on a hot summer day with this cool and refreshing salad, complete with tasty roasted red peppers, lime and a sprinkle of fresh Parmesan.

Roasted red peppers, blotted dry	1/2 cup	125 mL
Balsamic vinaigrette dressing	1/4 cup	60 mL
Lime juice	2 tbsp.	30 mL
Garlic clove, minced	1	1
(or 1/4 tsp., 1 mL, powder)		
Salt	1/4 tsp.	1 mL
Pepper	1/4 tsp.	1 mL
Can of lentils, rinsed and drained	19 oz.	540 mL
Chopped tomato	1 1/2 cups	375 mL
Chopped green pepper	1 cup	250 mL
Sliced green onion	1/2 cup	125 mL
Grated Parmesan cheese	2 tbsp.	30 mL

Process first 6 ingredients in blender or food processor until smooth. Transfer to large bowl.

Add next 4 ingredients. Stir.

Sprinkle with cheese. Makes about 4 1/2 cups (1.1 L).

1 cup (250 mL): 184 Calories; 4.7 g Total Fat (trace Mono, 0.1 g Poly, 1.2 g Sat); 3 mg Cholesterol; 25 g Carbohydrate; 10 g Fibre; 10 g Protein; 587 mg Sodium

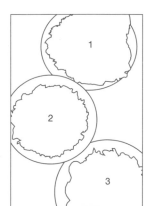

1. Fruity Rice and Pork, page 118
2. Moroccan Wild Rice Salad, page 96
3. Mediterranean White Bean Salad, page 117

Props: Jars

Winter Lentil Salad

A bowlful of flavour to enjoy during colder weather! The texture of chewy lentils contrasts nicely with crunchy apples and peppers, and a topping of feta makes an eye-catching garnish.

Fresh medium unpeeled beet, scrubbed clean and trimmed (see Note)	1	1
Can of lentils, rinsed and drained	19 oz.	540 mL
Chopped unpeeled cooking apple (such as McIntosh)	2 cups	500 mL
Chopped yellow pepper	1/2 cup	125 mL
Chopped fresh parsley	1/4 cup	60 mL
Cooking oil	3 tbsp.	50 mL
Lemon juice	3 tbsp.	50 mL
Thinly sliced green onion	3 tbsp.	50 mL
White wine vinegar	4 tsp.	20 mL
Dijon mustard	1 1/2 tsp.	7 mL
Granulated sugar	1 1/2 tsp.	7 mL
Salt	1/2 tsp.	2 mL
Pepper	1/4 tsp.	1 mL
Crumbled feta cheese	1/4 cup	60 mL

Place beet in small bowl. Microwave, covered, on high (100%) for about 4 minutes until tender. Let stand until cool. Transfer to cutting board. Peel. Cut into 1/2 inch (12 mm) pieces. Transfer to large bowl.

Add next 4 ingredients.

Whisk next 8 ingredients in separate small bowl. Add to beet mixture. Stir.

Sprinkle with cheese. Makes about 6 cups (1.5 L).

1 cup (250 mL): 210 Calories; 9.0 g Total Fat (4.4 g Mono, 2.3 g Poly, 1.5 g Sat); 6 mg Cholesterol; 30 g Carbohydrate; 5 g Fibre; 10 g Protein; 302 mg Sodium

Note: Don't get caught red-handed! Wear rubber gloves when handling beets.

Cajun Fish Salad

Here's a real Southern-style treat, complete with black-eyed peas and veggies topped with spicy cornmeal-coated fish. The bean salad can be made in advance, and navy or white beans can be used in place of black-eyes peas.

Can of black-eyed peas, rinsed and drained	19 oz.	540 mL
Chopped tomato	1 cup	250 mL
Frozen kernel corn, thawed	1 cup	250 mL
Chopped celery	1/2 cup	125 mL
Chopped green pepper	1/2 cup	125 mL
Chopped red pepper	1/2 cup	125 mL
Sun-dried tomato dressing	1/3 cup	75 mL
Chopped red onion	1/4 cup	60 mL
Chopped fresh thyme (or 1/2 tsp., 2 mL, dried)	2 tsp.	10 mL
Salt	1/2 tsp.	2 mL
Pepper	1/4 tsp.	1 mL
Yellow cornmeal	1/3 cup	75 mL
Cajun seasoning	2 tbsp.	30 mL
Salt	1/8 tsp.	0.5 mL
Tilapia fillets, any small bones removed	1 lb.	454 g
Cooking oil	1 tbsp.	15 mL
Cut or torn green leaf lettuce, lightly packed	2 cups	500 mL

Toss first 11 ingredients in large bowl.

Combine next 3 ingredients in medium shallow dish.

Press both sides of fillets into cornmeal mixture until coated. Discard any remaining cornmeal mixture. Heat cooking oil in large frying pan on medium-high. Add fillets. Cook for about 2 minutes per side until fish flakes easily when tested with fork.

Arrange lettuce on 4 serving plates. Spoon black-eyed pea mixture over lettuce. Top with fillets. Serves 4.

1 serving: 343 Calories; 9.4 g Total Fat (2.6 g Mono, 1.7 g Poly, 1.3 g Sat); 57 mg Cholesterol; 38 g Carbohydrate; 8 g Fibre; 32 g Protein; 1993 mg Sodium

Variation: Break fish into smaller pieces and arrange over black-eyed pea mixture.

California Roll Salad

Get your sushi fix without the rolling and slicing! Nutty brown rice blends with favourite California roll flavours—crisp cucumber, crab, wasabi, pickled ginger and nori—to create a creamy, satisfying salad.

Water	1 1/3 cups	325 mL
Salt	1/8 tsp.	0.5 mL
Long-grain brown rice	2/3 cup	150 mL
Chopped imitation crabmeat (1/2 inch, 12 mm, pieces)	2 cups	500 mL
Chopped English cucumber (with peel), 1/2 inch (12 mm) pieces	1 cup	250 mL
Julienned carrot	1/3 cup	75 mL
Slivered red pepper	1/3 cup	75 mL
Chopped pickled ginger slices	1 tbsp.	15 mL
Salt	1/2 tsp.	2 mL
Nori (roasted seaweed) sheet	1	1
Mayonnaise	1/4 cup	60 mL
Rice vinegar	2 tbsp.	30 mL
Granulated sugar	1 tbsp.	15 mL
Sesame seeds, toasted (see Tip, page 134)	1 1/2 tsp.	7 mL
Soy sauce	1 tsp.	5 mL
Wasabi paste (Japanese horseradish)	1/2 tsp.	2 mL
Romaine and iceberg lettuce mix	4 cups	1 L
Thinly sliced green onion	2 tbsp.	30 mL

Combine water and salt in small saucepan. Bring to a boil. Add rice. Stir. Reduce heat to medium-low. Simmer, covered, for about 35 minutes, without stirring, until rice is tender. Remove from heat. Let stand, covered, for about 5 minutes until liquid is absorbed. Transfer to large bowl. Cool.

Add next 6 ingredients.

Cut nori into 2 inch (5 cm) strips. Stack strips. Cut crosswise into 1/4 inch (6 mm) strips. Add to rice mixture.

Whisk next 6 ingredients in small bowl until sugar is dissolved. Add to rice mixture. Stir.

(continued on next page)

Legumes & Grains

Arrange lettuce in 4 salad bowls. Spoon rice mixture over lettuce. Sprinkle with green onion. Serves 4.

1 cup (250 mL): 330 Calories; 13.5 g Total Fat (0.5 g Mono, 0.7 g Poly, 1.9 g Sat); 65 mg Cholesterol; 33 g Carbohydrate; 3 g Fibre; 18 g Protein; 878 mg Sodium

Pictured on page 89.

African Chickpea Salad

Flavourful chickpeas, tuna and avocado provide complementary textures in this delicious blend, based on a traditional African salad.

Thinly sliced onion	1/4 cup	60 mL
Apple cider vinegar	1/4 cup	60 mL
Can of chickpeas (garbanzo beans), rinsed and drained	19 oz.	540 mL
Can of flaked light tuna in water, drained	6 oz.	170 g
Canned kernel corn	1/2 cup	125 mL
Diced avocado	1/2 cup	125 mL
Diced red pepper	1/3 cup	75 mL
Salad dressing (or mayonnaise)	1/3 cup	75 mL
Milk	1 tbsp.	15 mL
Granulated sugar	1/2 tsp.	2 mL
Cayenne pepper	1/8 tsp.	0.5 mL
Romaine lettuce heart leaves	16	16
Slices of English cucumber (with peel)	16	16
Roma (plum) tomatoes, quartered	4	4
Salted peanuts, coarsely chopped	1/4 cup	60 mL

Combine onion and vinegar in large bowl. Let stand for 30 minutes. Drain and discard vinegar.

Add next 5 ingredients.

Combine next 4 ingredients in small bowl. Add to chickpea mixture. Stir.

Arrange lettuce on 4 serving plates. Spoon chickpea mixture over lettuce. Arrange cucumber and tomato around chickpea mixture. Sprinkle with peanuts. Serves 4.

1 serving: 455 Calories; 26.4 g Total Fat (2.7 g Mono, 2.0 g Poly, 4.1 g Sat); 25 mg Cholesterol; 34 g Carbohydrate; 10 g Fibre; 21 g Protein; 571 mg Sodium

Pictured on page 18.

Lemon Walnut Scallop Salad

The nutty flavours of brown rice and walnuts are brightened with a zesty lemon and Dijon dressing, sweet bay scallops and grape tomatoes.

Water	2 cups	500 mL
Salt	3/4 tsp.	4 mL
Long-grain brown rice	1 cup	250 mL
Diced yellow pepper	1 cup	250 mL
Sliced grape tomatoes	1 cup	250 mL
Chopped fresh parsley	2 tbsp.	30 mL
(or 1 1/2 tsp., 7 mL, dried)		
Olive oil	1/3 cup	75 mL
Walnut pieces, toasted (see Tip, page 134)	1/4 cup	60 mL
Lemon juice	2 tbsp.	30 mL
Dijon mustard (with whole seeds)	1 tsp.	5 mL
Grated lemon zest	1 tsp.	5 mL
Salt	1/4 tsp.	1 mL
Pepper	1/4 tsp.	1 mL
Olive (or cooking) oil	1 tsp.	5 mL
Small bay scallops	3/4 lb.	340 g
Walnut pieces, toasted (see Tip, page 134)	1/4 cup	60 mL

Combine water and salt in medium saucepan. Bring to a boil. Add rice. Stir. Reduce heat to medium-low. Simmer, covered, for about 35 minutes, without stirring, until rice is tender. Remove from heat. Let stand, covered, for about 5 minutes until liquid is absorbed. Fluff with fork. Transfer to large bowl. Cool.

Add next 3 ingredients.

Process next 7 ingredients in blender or food processor until smooth. Add to rice mixture. Stir.

Heat second amount of olive oil in large frying pan on medium-high. Add scallops. Cook for about 3 minutes, stirring occasionally, until scallops are opaque. Add to rice mixture. Toss gently.

Sprinkle with second amount of walnuts. Makes about 7 cups (1.75 L).

1 cup (250 mL): 306 Calories; 18.2 g Total Fat (9.2 g Mono, 6.1 g Poly, 2.4 g Sat); 16 mg Cholesterol; 26 g Carbohydrate; 2 g Fibre; 12 g Protein; 429 mg Sodium

Curried Rice Paneer Salad

Golden rice with a hint of curry and a sweet ginger dressing. Paneer is a fresh cheese available frozen in some grocery stores or fresh in Indian markets. A mild cheese such as farmer's or bocconcini can be used instead.

Water	2 cups	500 mL
Curry powder	1 tsp.	5 mL
Salt	1/8 tsp.	0.5 mL
White basmati rice	1 cup	250 mL
Can of chickpeas (garbanzo beans), rinsed and drained	19 oz.	540 mL
Diced paneer	2 cups	500 mL
Diced orange pepper	1 cup	250 mL
Frozen tiny peas, thawed	1 cup	250 mL
Chopped fresh cilantro (or parsley)	3 tbsp.	50 mL
SWEET GINGER VINAIGRETTE		
Lime juice	6 tbsp.	100 mL
Cooking oil	1/4 cup	60 mL
Liquid honey	1/4 cup	60 mL
Finely grated ginger root	2 tbsp.	30 mL
Curry powder	2 tsp.	10 mL
Garlic clove, minced (or 1/2 tsp., 2 mL, powder)	2	2
Salt	1 tsp.	5 mL
Pepper	1/8 tsp.	0.5 mL

Combine first 3 ingredients in medium saucepan. Bring to a boil. Add rice. Stir. Reduce heat to medium-low. Simmer, covered, for 15 minutes, without stirring. Remove from heat. Let stand, covered, for about 5 minutes until rice is tender and liquid is absorbed. Fluff with fork. Transfer to large bowl. Cool.

Add next 5 ingredients.

Sweet Ginger Vinaigrette: Whisk all 8 ingredients in small bowl. Makes about 1 cup (250 mL). Add to rice mixture. Stir. Makes about 9 cups (2.25 L).

1 cup (250 mL): 317 Calories; 14.4 g Total Fat (3.8 g Mono, 2.3 g Poly, 4.9 g Sat); 27 mg Cholesterol; 37 g Carbohydrate; 4 g Fibre; 11 g Protein; 390 mg Sodium

Olé Barley Salad

Pearl barley makes a great backdrop for colourful vegetables and black olives in this spicy vegetarian meal salad, rich with Mexican-style flavours.

Water	3 cups	750 mL
Pearl barley, rinsed and drained	1 cup	250 mL
Chopped tomato	1 cup	250 mL
Grated Monterey Jack cheese	1 cup	250 mL
Diced yellow pepper	2/3 cup	150 mL
Chopped fresh cilantro (or parsley)	1/3 cup	75 mL
Sliced black olives	1/3 cup	75 mL
Sliced green onion	1/3 cup	75 mL

SPICY VINAIGRETTE

Cooking oil	3 tbsp.	50 mL
Lime juice	3 tbsp.	50 mL
Granulated sugar	2 tsp.	10 mL
Ground cumin	1/2 tsp.	2 mL
Hot pepper sauce	1/2 tsp.	2 mL
Salt	1 tsp.	5 mL
Pepper	1/4 tsp.	1 mL

Pour water into medium saucepan. Bring to a boil. Add barley. Stir. Reduce heat to medium-low. Simmer, covered, for about 25 minutes until barley is tender. Drain. Transfer to large bowl. Cool.

Add next 6 ingredients.

Spicy Vinaigrette: Whisk all 7 ingredients in small bowl. Makes about 1/2 cup (125 mL). Drizzle over barley mixture. Stir. Makes about 5 1/3 cups (1.3 L).

1 cup (250 mL): 309 Calories; 16.5 g Total Fat (5.2 g Mono, 2.4 g Poly, 4.5 g Sat); 19 mg Cholesterol; 36 g Carbohydrate; 7 g Fibre; 9 g Protein; 670 mg Sodium

Pictured on page 36.

Mediterranean White Bean Salad

Enjoy rich Mediterranean flavours paired with nutritious white beans for a hearty, well-rounded meal salad. With minimal prep work, it's a snap to put together.

Olive (or cooking) oil	1/3 cup	75 mL
Balsamic vinegar	1 tbsp.	15 mL
Lemon juice	1 tbsp.	15 mL
Dried thyme	1 tsp.	5 mL
Grated lemon zest	1 tsp.	5 mL
Liquid honey	1 tsp.	5 mL
Garlic clove, minced	1	1
(or 1/4 tsp., 1 mL, powder)		
Salt	1/4 tsp.	1 mL
Pepper	1/4 tsp.	1 mL
Cans of white kidney beans (19 oz.,	2	2
540 mL, each), rinsed and drained		
Jars of marinated artichoke hearts,	2	2
(6 oz., 170 mL, each), drained,		
quartered		
Jar of roasted red peppers, drained,	12 oz.	340 mL
cut into strips		
Cherry tomatoes, halved	2 cups	500 mL
Thinly sliced red onion	1/2 cup	125 mL
Chopped fresh basil	2 tbsp.	30 mL
Chopped fresh parsley	2 tbsp.	30 mL

Whisk first 9 ingredients in small bowl.

Combine remaining 7 ingredients in large bowl. Drizzle olive oil mixture over top. Stir gently. Makes about 7 1/2 cups (1.9 L).

1 cup (250 mL): 287 Calories; 11.2 g Total Fat (7.1 g Mono, 1.5 g Poly, 1.4 g Sat); 0 mg Cholesterol; 34 g Carbohydrate; 6 g Fibre; 10 g Protein; 692 mg Sodium

Pictured on page 108.

Fruity Rice and Pork

There is a Polynesian feel to this summer salad, whose flavours marinate overnight. A tangy pineapple, kiwi and rice blend is spooned over crisp lettuce and topped with sesame seed-crusted pork.

Thick teriyaki basting sauce	2/3 cup	150 mL
Ginger marmalade	1/2 cup	125 mL
Pork tenderloin, trimmed of fat	1 lb.	454 g
Sesame seeds, toasted (see Tip, page 134)	1/2 cup	125 mL
Water	2 cups	500 mL
Salt	1/2 tsp.	2 mL
Jasmine rice	1 cup	250 mL
Can of pineapple tidbits, drained	14 oz.	398 mL
Diced kiwifruit	1 cup	250 mL
Diced red onion	1/4 cup	60 mL
Asian-style sesame dressing	1/4 cup	60 mL
Apple cider vinegar	1 tbsp.	15 mL
Red leaf lettuce leaves	8	8

Process teriyaki sauce and marmalade in blender until smooth. Transfer 1/4 cup (60 mL) to small bowl. Chill.

Place tenderloin in large resealable freezer bag. Pour remaining teriyaki mixture over tenderloin. Seal bag. Turn until coated. Marinate in refrigerator for at least 6 hours or overnight. Remove tenderloin. Discard any remaining teriyaki mixture.

Spread sesame seeds on large plate. Press tenderloin into sesame seeds until coated. Discard any remaining sesame seeds. Place on greased baking sheet. Bake in 400°F (205°C) oven for about 30 minutes until internal temperature reaches 155°F (68°C). Transfer to cutting board. Cover with foil. Let stand for 10 minutes. Internal temperature should rise to at least 160°F (71°C). Slice thinly.

(continued on next page)

Combine water and salt in medium saucepan. Bring to a boil. Add rice. Stir. Reduce heat to medium-low. Simmer, covered, for 15 minutes, without stirring. Remove from heat. Let stand, covered, for about 5 minutes until rice is tender and liquid is absorbed. Fluff with fork. Transfer to large bowl. Let stand until cool.

Add next 3 ingredients. Stir.

Add dressing and vinegar to reserved teriyaki mixture. Whisk. Drizzle over rice mixture. Stir.

Arrange lettuce on 4 serving plates. Spoon rice mixture over lettuce. Top with pork. Serves 4.

1 serving: 543 Calories; 16.0 g Total Fat (1.8 g Mono, 0.6 g Poly, 1.9 g Sat); 74 mg Cholesterol; 66 g Carbohydrate; 3 g Fibre; 30 g Protein; 1003 mg Sodium

Pictured on page 108.

Paré Pointer

Knock knock.

Who's there?

Boo.

Boo who?

Aw - don't cry.

Reuben Slaw

For fans of the Reuben sandwich, and those new to it too! A fun take on the sandwich classic with slivered pastrami, grilled Swiss cheese croutons and tangy sauerkraut.

SWISS CROUTONS

Butter (or hard margarine), softened	1 tbsp.	15 mL
Rye bread slices	6	6
Swiss cheese slices (1 oz., 28 g, each)	3	3

DELI SLAW

Grated (or julienned) carrot	1 cup	250 mL
Grated unpeeled tart apple (such as Granny Smith)	1 cup	250 mL
Shredded red cabbage, lightly packed	1 cup	250 mL
Wine sauerkraut, drained	1 cup	250 mL
Thousand Island dressing	1/3 cup	75 mL
Shaved pastrami (or smoked meat), cut into thin strips	4 oz.	113 g
Chopped dill pickles	1/4 cup	60 mL

Swiss Croutons: Spread butter over each bread slice. Arrange 3 bread slices, butter-side down, in large frying pan on medium. Place 1 cheese slice on each. Top with remaining bread slices, butter-side up. Cook for about 3 minutes per side until bread is golden and cheese is melted. Transfer to cutting board. Let stand for 5 minutes. Cut into 1 inch (2.5 cm) pieces.

Deli Slaw: Combine first 5 ingredients in large bowl. Makes about 4 cups (1 L). Transfer to 4 serving plates.

Top with pastrami, pickles and Swiss Croutons. Serves 4.

1 serving: 421 Calories; 19.2 g Total Fat (1.4 g Mono, 0.6 g Poly, 7.6 g Sat); 54 mg Cholesterol; 44 g Carbohydrate; 5 g Fibre; 18 g Protein; 1336 mg Sodium

Pictured on page 125.

Paré Pointer

It's best not to believe political jokes. Too many get elected.

Sweet Ginger Beef Slaw

Now you can have a crisp, gingery stir-fry without the deep frying! This salad is packed with the fresh Asian flavours of crunchy veggies and sweet gingery beef.

Brown sugar, packed	2 tbsp.	30 mL
Soy sauce	2 tbsp.	30 mL
Finely grated ginger root	1 tbsp.	15 mL
(or 3/4 tsp., 4 mL, ground ginger)		
Garlic cloves, minced	2	2
(or 1/2 tsp., 2 mL, powder)		
Pepper	1/8 tsp.	0.5 mL
Sesame (or cooking) oil	1 tsp.	5 mL
Beef top sirloin steak, cut into thin strips	1 lb.	454 g
Sesame seeds, toasted (see Tip, page 134)	2 tbsp.	30 mL
Broccoli slaw (or shredded cabbage with carrot), lightly packed	4 cups	1 L
Can of cut baby corn, drained	14 oz.	398 mL
Snow peas, trimmed and halved diagonally	1 cup	250 mL
Asian-style sesame dressing	1/2 cup	125 mL
Julienned radish	1/2 cup	125 mL
Finely sliced green onion	2 tbsp.	30 mL

Combine first 5 ingredients in small cup.

Heat large frying pan or wok on medium-high until very hot. Add sesame oil. Add beef. Stir-fry for about 4 minutes until browned. Add brown sugar mixture. Stir. Cook for about 1 minute, stirring often, until coated. Remove from heat.

Sprinkle with sesame seeds. Toss. Let stand for 10 minutes.

Combine remaining 6 ingredients in extra-large bowl. Add beef. Toss. Makes about 10 1/2 cups (2.6 L).

1 1/2 cups (375 mL): 276 Calories; 11.2 g Total Fat (2.1 g Mono, 0.6 g Poly, 2.6 g Sat); 35 mg Cholesterol; 28 g Carbohydrate; 3 g Fibre; 18 g Protein; 614 mg Sodium

Pictured on page 125.

Fennel Chicken Slaw

This light meal salad combines the crunch of a traditional cabbage slaw with tart apple and the mild licorice flavour of fennel, all bathed in a creamy lemon dressing.

Plain yogurt	1/2 cup	125 mL
Buttermilk	2 tbsp.	30 mL
Chopped fresh chives (or green onion)	1 tbsp.	15 mL
Liquid honey	1 tbsp.	15 mL
Fennel seed, bruised and toasted (see Note)	1 tsp.	5 mL
Grated lemon zest	1 tsp.	5 mL
Salt	1/2 tsp.	2 mL
Pepper	1/2 tsp.	2 mL
Grated unpeeled tart apple (such as Granny Smith)	2 cups	500 mL
Lemon juice	2 tbsp.	30 mL
Thinly sliced fennel bulb (white part only)	4 cups	1 L
Chopped cooked chicken (see Tip, page 41)	2 cups	500 mL
Grated carrot	1 1/2 cups	375 mL
Chopped fresh parsley	2 tbsp.	30 mL

Whisk first 8 ingredients in small bowl.

Combine apple and lemon juice in large bowl.

Add remaining 4 ingredients. Add yogurt mixture. Toss. Chill, covered, for 1 hour to blend flavours. Makes about 8 cups (2 L).

1 cup (250 mL): 126 Calories; 2.9 g Total Fat (1.0 g Mono, 0.6 g Poly, 0.8 g Sat); 32 mg Cholesterol; 14 g Carbohydrate; 3 g Fibre; 12 g Protein; 231 mg Sodium

Note: To bruise fennel seed, pound with mallet or press with flat side of knife to "bruise" or crack open seeds. To toast fennel seed, place seeds in an ungreased shallow frying pan. Heat on medium for about 2 minutes, stirring often, until golden.

Spicy Hoisin Chicken Slaw

Spiced-up chicken is paired with Asian vegetables for a colourful slaw. A warm lunch or dinner with plenty of crunchy appeal.

Prepared chicken broth	1/4 cup	60 mL
Hoisin sauce	3 tbsp.	50 mL
Liquid honey	1 tbsp.	15 mL
Chili paste (sambal oelek)	2 tsp.	10 mL
Boneless, skinless chicken thighs, cut into 3/4 inch (2 cm) pieces	3/4 lb.	340 g
Garlic clove, minced (or 1/4 tsp., 1 mL, powder)	1	1
White vinegar	3 tbsp.	50 mL
Cornstarch	1 tsp.	5 mL
Cooking oil	1 tbsp.	15 mL
Shredded suey choy (Chinese cabbage), lightly packed	6 cups	1.5 L
Fresh bean sprouts	1 1/2 cups	375 mL
Snow peas, trimmed and slivered	2/3 cup	150 mL
Julienned carrot	1/2 cup	125 mL
Slivered red pepper	1/2 cup	125 mL
Thinly sliced red onion	1/2 cup	125 mL
Sesame seeds, toasted (see Tip, page 134)	2 tbsp.	30 mL

Combine first 4 ingredients in small bowl.

Combine chicken and garlic in medium bowl. Add 1/4 cup (60 mL) broth mixture. Stir until coated. Marinate, covered, in refrigerator for 20 minutes.

Add vinegar and cornstarch to remaining broth mixture. Stir.

Heat large frying pan or wok on medium-high until very hot. Add cooking oil. Add chicken mixture. Stir-fry for about 4 minutes until chicken is no longer pink inside. Stir broth mixture. Add to chicken mixture. Heat and stir for about 30 seconds until boiling and slightly thickened.

Toss remaining 7 ingredients in extra-large bowl. Add chicken mixture. Toss. Serve immediately. Makes about 10 cups (2.5 L).

1 1/2 cups (375 mL): 173 Calories; 7.5 g Total Fat (2.7 g Mono, 1.6 g Poly, 1.3 g Sat); 33 mg Cholesterol; 15 g Carbohydrate; 2 g Fibre; 12 g Protein; 408 mg Sodium

Pictured on page 125.

Peppy Salad Pizza

Fun tortilla crisps surround a salad with "the works"! Crowd-pleasing pizza flavours are perfect for a themed or casual party for all ages. If you don't have a round platter, use your pizza pan.

Pizza sauce	1/4 cup	60 mL
Flour tortillas (9 inch, 22 cm, diameter)	2	2
Italian dressing	1/3 cup	75 mL
Pizza sauce	2 tbsp.	30 mL
Dried oregano	1/4 tsp.	1 mL
Shredded iceberg lettuce, lightly packed	4 cups	1 L
Chopped deli pepperoni slices	1 cup	250 mL
Chopped green pepper	1 cup	250 mL
Sliced fresh white mushrooms	1 cup	250 mL
Tomato slices	8	8
Grated Italian cheese blend	1/2 cup	125 mL
Sliced black olives	1/4 cup	60 mL

Brush 2 tbsp. (30 mL) pizza sauce onto each tortilla. Cut each tortilla into 12 wedges. Arrange in single layer on greased baking sheet. Bake in 350°F (175°C) oven for about 15 minutes until crisp and golden.

Combine next 3 ingredients in large bowl. Add next 4 ingredients. Toss. Transfer to round serving platter.

Layer remaining 3 ingredients, in order given, over top. Arrange tortilla triangles around edge of platter. Serve immediately. Serves 4.

1 serving: 469 Calories; 38.5 g Total Fat (0.7 g Mono, 0.2 g Poly, 12.1 g Sat); 54 mg Cholesterol; 19 g Carbohydrate; 3 g Fibre; 18 g Protein; 1639 mg Sodium

Pictured on page 143.

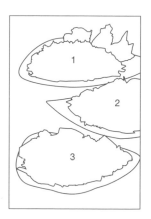

1. Spicy Hoisin Chicken Slaw, page 123
2. Sweet Ginger Beef Slaw, page 121
3. Reuben Slaw, page 120

Buffalo Chicken Coleslaw

Satisfy your craving for buffalo chicken wings—by eating salad! The flavours of buffalo chicken wings, carrot and celery sticks and blue cheese dressing are combined in this crunchy coleslaw.

Cooking oil	2 tsp.	10 mL
Boneless, skinless chicken breast halves, cut into 1/2 inch (12 mm) pieces	3/4 lb.	340 g
Louisiana hot sauce	1 tbsp.	15 mL
Coleslaw mix, lightly packed	4 cups	1 L
Grated Monterey Jack cheese	1 1/2 cups	375 mL
Diced celery	1 cup	250 mL
Salad dressing (or mayonnaise)	1/3 cup	75 mL
Blue cheese dressing	1/4 cup	60 mL
Granulated sugar	1 tsp.	5 mL
Louisiana hot sauce	1 tsp.	5 mL

Heat cooking oil in large frying pan on medium-high. Add chicken. Cook for about 5 minutes, stirring occasionally, until browned. Add hot sauce. Cook for about 3 minutes, stirring often, until no longer pink inside. Transfer to large bowl. Let stand until cool.

Add next 3 ingredients. Toss.

Combine remaining 4 ingredients in small bowl. Add to coleslaw mixture. Stir. Chill, covered, for 2 hours to blend flavours. Makes about 6 cups (1.5 L).

1 cup (250 mL): 343 Calories; 26.5 g Total Fat (2.8 g Mono, 3.7 g Poly, 7.9 g Sat); 64 mg Cholesterol; 7 g Carbohydrate; 2 g Fibre; 19 g Protein; 515 mg Sodium

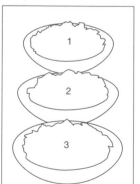

1. Chicken Taco Layers, page 129
2. Marinated Asian Vegetable Salad, page 133
3. Layered Orzo Salad, page 130

Layered Paella Salad

This paella (pi-AY-yuh) is a big, vibrant meal salad for seafood lovers!
A shrimp and scallop medley also works in place of the frozen seafood mix.
Chill the dressed seafood blend and rice separately overnight.

Prepared vegetable broth	3 cups	750 mL
Frozen seafood mix, thawed	1 lb.	454 g
Lemon juice	1/4 cup	60 mL
Olive (or cooking) oil	1/4 cup	60 mL
Chopped fresh parsley	2 tbsp.	30 mL
Granulated sugar	2 tsp.	10 mL
Grated lemon zest	2 tsp.	10 mL
Smoked sweet paprika (or chili powder)	1 tsp.	5 mL
Salt	1/2 tsp.	2 mL
Pepper	1/4 tsp.	1 mL
Water		
Package of Spanish-style rice mix	14 oz.	397 g
Olive (or cooking) oil	1 tbsp.	15 mL
Cut or torn green leaf lettuce, lightly packed	6 cups	1.5 L
Chopped green pepper	1 1/2 cups	375 mL
Chopped red pepper	1 1/2 cups	375 mL
Frozen tiny peas, thawed	1 1/2 cups	375 mL
Thinly sliced red onion	1/2 cup	125 mL

Pour broth into medium saucepan. Bring to a boil. Add seafood mix. Heat and stir for about 2 minutes until seafood is cooked. Transfer seafood with slotted spoon to medium bowl. Transfer broth to large measuring cup.

Whisk next 8 ingredients in small bowl until sugar is dissolved. Add to seafood. Stir until coated. Marinate, covered, in refrigerator for at least 6 hours or overnight, stirring occasionally.

Add water to reserved broth, if necessary, to make 3 1/2 cups (875 mL). Pour into large saucepan. Add rice mix and second amount of olive oil. Bring to a boil. Stir. Reduce heat to medium-low. Simmer, covered, for 10 minutes, without stirring. Remove from heat. Let stand, covered, for about 5 minutes until rice is tender and liquid is absorbed. Cool. Chill, covered, for at least 6 hours or overnight.

(continued on next page)

Arrange lettuce in extra-large shallow bowl or platter. Spoon rice mixture over lettuce. Layer remaining 4 ingredients, in order given, over rice. Stir seafood mixture. Spoon over top. Makes about 14 cups (3.5 L).

1 1/2 cups (375 mL): 300 Calories; 8.6 g Total Fat (5.4 g Mono, 1.3 g Poly, 1.2 g Sat); 62 mg Cholesterol; 45 g Carbohydrate; 4 g Fibre; 13 g Protein; 983 mg Sodium

Pictured on page 143.

Chicken Taco Layers

This easy layered salad will be a sure hit. It features everyone's favourite Mexican flavours, all dressed in a delicious lime and sour cream blend.

Shredded iceberg lettuce, lightly packed	4 cups	1 L
Chopped cooked chicken (see Tip, page 41)	2 cups	500 mL
Medium salsa	1/2 cup	125 mL
Chopped avocado	2 cups	500 mL
Chopped tomato	2 cups	500 mL
Chopped green onion	3/4 cup	175 mL
Grated Mexican cheese blend	1 cup	250 mL
Sour cream	1/2 cup	125 mL
Chopped fresh jalapeño peppers (see Tip, page 81)	2 tbsp.	30 mL
Lime juice	2 tbsp.	30 mL
Chopped fresh cilantro (or parsley)	1 tbsp.	15 mL
Olive (or cooking) oil	1 tbsp.	15 mL
Salt	1/2 tsp.	2 mL
Crushed tortilla chips	1 cup	250 mL

Arrange lettuce in extra-large glass bowl.

Combine chicken and salsa in medium bowl. Spoon over lettuce.

Layer next 4 ingredients, in order given, over chicken mixture.

Process next 6 ingredients in blender until smooth. Drizzle over cheese.

Scatter tortilla chips over top. Makes about 13 cups (3.25 L).

1 1/2 cups (375 mL): 263 Calories; 17.4 g Total Fat (5.9 g Mono, 2.0 g Poly, 5.9 g Sat); 49 mg Cholesterol; 13 g Carbohydrate; 3 g Fibre; 14 g Protein; 415 mg Sodium

Pictured on page 126.

Layered Orzo Salad

A guest-worthy meal salad, this attractive, colourful blend has flavours reminiscent of bruschetta. Crisp vegetables paired with orzo and cheese add delicious contrast.

Water	8 cups	2 L
Salt	1 tsp.	5 mL
Orzo	1 cup	250 mL
Italian dressing	3 tbsp.	50 mL
Chopped bocconcini (or diced mozzarella cheese)	2 cups	500 mL
Chopped tomato	2 cups	500 mL
Chopped fresh basil	1/4 cup	60 mL
Pepper	1/2 tsp.	10 mL
Romaine, radicchio and endive mix, lightly packed	4 cups	1 L
Grated Parmesan cheese	1/4 cup	60 mL
Italian dressing	1/4 cup	60 mL
Diced English cucumber (with peel)	1 cup	250 mL
Roasted red peppers, cut into strips	1 cup	250 mL
Sliced pitted kalamata olives	1/2 cup	125 mL
Grated Parmesan cheese	1/4 cup	60 mL

Combine water and salt in large saucepan. Bring to a boil. Add pasta. Boil, uncovered, for 8 to 10 minutes, stirring occasionally, until tender but firm. Drain. Rinse with cold water. Drain well. Return to saucepan.

Add first amount of dressing. Stir. Spoon into extra-large glass bowl.

Combine next 4 ingredients in large bowl. Spoon over orzo mixture.

Combine next 3 ingredients in same large bowl. Arrange over bocconcini mixture.

Scatter next 3 ingredients, in order given, over lettuce mixture. Sprinkle with second amount of Parmesan cheese. Makes about 12 cups (3 L).

1 1/2 cups (375 mL): 330 Calories; 20.1 g Total Fat (trace Mono, 0.1 g Poly, 6.0 g Sat); 28 mg Cholesterol; 22 g Carbohydrate; 2 g Fibre; 17 g Protein; 553 mg Sodium

Pictured on page 126.

Cucumber Tabbouleh Salad

Lebanese-style layered salad becomes a meal with the addition of garlicky hummus, and can be served with pita wedges or chips. Lemon, olive oil and parsley add wonderful freshness.

Boiling water	3/4 cup	175 mL
Bulgur, fine grind	1/2 cup	125 mL
Lemon juice	1/2 cup	125 mL
Olive oil	1/3 cup	75 mL
Salt	1 tsp.	5 mL
Pepper	1/2 tsp.	2 mL
Cut or torn romaine lettuce, lightly packed	4 cups	1 L
Hummus	1 1/2 cups	375 mL
Finely chopped fresh parsley	2 1/2 cups	625 mL
Chopped fresh mint	1/2 cup	125 mL
Finely chopped red onion	1/4 cup	60 mL
Chopped English cucumber (with peel)	1 1/2 cups	375 mL
Chopped seeded tomato	1 1/2 cups	375 mL

Combine boiling water and bulgur in small heat-proof bowl. Let stand, covered, for about 20 minutes until tender. Drain well. Transfer to large bowl.

Whisk next 4 ingredients in small bowl.

Arrange lettuce in extra-large glass bowl. Spoon hummus evenly over lettuce.

Add next 3 ingredients and 1/3 cup (75 mL) lemon juice mixture to bulgur. Stir. Spoon over hummus.

Layer cucumber and tomato over parsley mixture. Drizzle with remaining lemon juice mixture. Makes about 12 cups (3 L).

1 1/2 cups (375 mL): 216 Calories; 14.3 g Total Fat (8.6 g Mono, 3.2 g Poly, 2.1 g Sat); 0 mg Cholesterol; 20 g Carbohydrate; 6 g Fibre; 6 g Protein; 485 mg Sodium

Paré Pointer

To learn more about eggs, look in the hen-cyclopedia.

Crabby Spuds Salad

This creamy potato salad has a seafood flavour twist—crab and kernel corn offer sweetness to this rich and filling meal salad.

Baby potatoes, quartered	1 1/2 lbs.	680 g
Salt	1/2 tsp.	2 mL
Cooking oil	2 tsp.	10 mL
Frozen kernel corn	1 1/2 cups	375 mL
Garlic clove, minced	1	1
(or 1/4 tsp., 1 mL, powder)		
Chopped imitation crabmeat	2 cups	500 mL
Thinly sliced celery	3/4 cup	175 mL
Sliced green onion	1/3 cup	75 mL
Mayonnaise	3/4 cup	175 mL
Dijon mustard	4 tsp.	20 mL
White wine vinegar	4 tsp.	20 mL
Dried tarragon	1/4 tsp.	1 mL
Salt	1/8 tsp.	0.5 mL
Pepper	1/4 tsp.	1 mL

Pour water into large saucepan until about 1 inch (2.5 cm) deep. Add potato and salt. Cover. Bring to a boil. Reduce heat to medium. Boil gently for 12 to 15 minutes until tender. Drain. Rinse with cold water. Drain well. Transfer to large bowl.

Heat cooking oil in small frying pan on medium. Add corn and garlic. Cook for about 5 minutes, stirring occasionally, until corn is heated through. Cool. Add to potato.

Add next 3 ingredients. Stir gently.

Combine remaining 6 ingredients in small bowl. Add to potato mixture. Stir gently until coated. Makes about 6 cups (1.5 L).

1 cup (250 mL): 429 Calories; 24.3 g Total Fat (1.0 g Mono, 0.7 g Poly, 3.2 g Sat); 47 mg Cholesterol; 37 g Carbohydrate; 3 g Fibre; 14 g Protein; 329 mg Sodium

Paré Pointer

She thought a medicine dropper was a doctor with butterfingers.

Marinated Asian Vegetable Salad

Brightly coloured Asian vegetables provide plenty of crunch in this salad. Marinate overnight in a chili, sesame and ginger dressing and serve up using a slotted spoon, or drain before serving.

Water	3 cups	750 mL
Salt	1/2 tsp.	2 mL
Frozen shelled edamame (soy beans)	2 cups	500 mL
Can of cut baby corn, drained	14 oz.	398 mL
Package of firm tofu, cut into 1 inch (2.5 cm) cubes	12.75 oz.	350 g
Baby carrots, halved	1 cup	250 mL
Diagonally sliced celery (1 inch, 2.5 cm, pieces)	1 cup	250 mL
Diced red pepper	1 cup	250 mL
Grape tomatoes	1 cup	250 mL
Snow peas, trimmed and halved	1 cup	250 mL
Apple cider vinegar	1/3 cup	75 mL
Cooking oil	1/4 cup	60 mL
Fish sauce	4 tsp.	20 mL
Finely grated ginger root (or 3/4 tsp., 4 mL, powder)	1 tbsp.	15 mL
Granulated sugar	1 tbsp.	15 mL
Sesame oil (for flavour)	1 tbsp.	15 mL
Chili paste (sambal oelek)	2 tsp.	10 mL

Combine water and salt in medium saucepan. Bring to a boil. Add edamame. Reduce heat to medium. Boil gently, uncovered, for 5 minutes. Drain. Rinse with cold water. Drain well. Transfer to large bowl.

Add next 7 ingredients. Toss.

Whisk remaining 7 ingredients in small bowl. Add to edamame mixture. Toss. Chill for at least 6 hours or overnight, stirring occasionally. Makes about 9 cups (2.25 L).

1 cup (250 mL): 222 Calories; 12.4 g Total Fat (3.7 g Mono, 2.1 g Poly, 1.2 g Sat); 0 mg Cholesterol; 21 g Carbohydrate; 5 g Fibre; 10 g Protein; 275 mg Sodium

Pictured on page 126.

Roasted Fennel Salad

Here's a rustic fall salad for the adventurous crowd! Fennel, crunchy walnuts and goat cheese are tossed in a mildly sweet vinaigrette with a special ingredient—maple syrup.

Olive (or cooking) oil	3 tbsp.	50 mL
Lemon juice	2 tbsp.	30 mL
Maple syrup	2 tbsp.	30 mL
Balsamic vinegar	1 tbsp.	15 mL
Garlic powder	1/4 tsp.	1 mL
Salt	1/4 tsp.	1 mL
Pepper	1/4 tsp.	1 mL
Sliced fennel bulb (white part only), about 1/4 inch (6 mm) thick	8 cups	2 L
Cooking oil	1 tbsp.	15 mL
Romaine, radicchio and endive mix, lightly packed	6 cups	1.5 L
Goat (chèvre) cheese, cut up	3 oz.	85 g
Walnut pieces, toasted (see Tip, below)	1 cup	250 mL

Whisk first 7 ingredients in small bowl.

Combine fennel and cooking oil in large bowl. Arrange in single layer on greased baking sheet with sides. Bake in 425°F (220°C) oven for about 40 minutes until tender. Return to same large bowl. Cool.

Add lettuce and olive oil mixture. Toss.

Scatter cheese and walnuts over top. Makes about 7 cups (1.75 L).

1 cup (250 mL): 285 Calories; 20.8 g Total Fat (11.2 g Mono, 4.2 g Poly, 3.4 g Sat); 5 mg Cholesterol; 23 g Carbohydrate; 5 g Fibre; 6 g Protein; 291 mg Sodium

 tip When toasting nuts, seeds or coconut, cooking times will vary for each type of nut—so never toast them together. For small amounts, place ingredient in an ungreased shallow frying pan. Heat on medium for 3 to 5 minutes, stirring often, until golden. For larger amounts, spread ingredient evenly in an ungreased shallow pan. Bake in a 350°F (175°C) oven for 5 to 10 minutes, stirring or shaking often, until golden.

Greek Vegetable Salad

Find all the texture and bold flavour you'd expect in a Greek salad, with a hearty dressing that's chock full of puréed vegetables and herbs.

Can of chickpeas (garbanzo beans), rinsed and drained	19 oz.	540 mL
Chopped English cucumber (with peel), 3/4 inch (2 cm) pieces	2 cups	500 mL
Chopped green pepper (3/4 inch, 2 cm, pieces)	2 cups	500 mL
Halved cherry tomatoes	2 cups	500 mL
Diced feta cheese	1 cup	250 mL
Pitted kalamata olives	1 cup	250 mL
Diced red onion	1/2 cup	125 mL
VEGETABLE DRESSING		
Egg yolk (large), see Safety Tip, below	1	1
Chopped carrot	1/2 cup	125 mL
Chopped red onion	1/4 cup	60 mL
Olive (or cooking) oil	2 tbsp.	30 mL
Lemon juice	1 tbsp.	15 mL
Anchovy paste	2 tsp.	10 mL
Dried oregano	1 tsp.	5 mL
Granulated sugar	1 tsp.	5 mL
Celery salt	1/2 tsp.	2 mL
Garlic clove, minced (or 1/4 tsp., 1 mL, powder)	1	1

Toss first 7 ingredients in extra-large bowl.

Vegetable Dressing: Process all 10 ingredients in blender or food processor until well combined, but not smooth. Makes about 2/3 cup (150 mL). Add to cucumber mixture. Stir. Makes about 10 cups (2.5 L).

1 1/2 cups (375 mL): 233 Calories; 13.3 g Total Fat (6.2 g Mono, 1.8 g Poly, 4.5 g Sat); 51 mg Cholesterol; 22 g Carbohydrate; 6 g Fibre; 9 g Protein; 817 mg Sodium

Safety Tip: This recipe contains uncooked egg. Make sure to use fresh, clean Grade A eggs. Keep chilled and consume the same day the recipe is prepared. Always discard leftovers. Pregnant women, young children and the elderly are not advised to eat anything containing raw egg.

Pesto Veggie Steak Salad

Roasted veggies and juicy steak are tossed with fresh pesto for one deliciously filling meal salad! Round it out with garlic bread for an Italian-style meal.

Chopped red pepper (1 inch, 2.5 cm, pieces)	2 cups	500 mL
Chopped red onion (1 inch, 2.5 cm, pieces)	1 cup	250 mL
Medium zucchini (with peel), halved lengthwise and cut into 1/2 inch (12 mm) slices	1	1
Small Asian eggplant (with peel), halved lengthwise and cut into 1/2 inch (12 mm) slices	1	1
Olive (or cooking) oil	2 tbsp.	30 mL
Grape tomatoes, halved	2 cups	500 mL
Coarsely chopped fresh basil	1/2 cup	125 mL
Coarsely chopped fresh parsley	1/2 cup	125 mL
Grated Parmesan cheese	2 tbsp.	30 mL
Lemon juice	1 tbsp.	15 mL
Dijon mustard	1 tsp.	5 mL
Salt	1/2 tsp.	2 mL
Chopped garlic cloves	2	2
Olive (or cooking) oil	1/3 cup	75 mL
Flank steak	1 lb.	454 g
Salt, sprinkle		
Pepper, sprinkle		

Toss first 5 ingredients in greased 9 x 13 inch (22 x 33 cm) baking dish. Bake in 425°F (220°C) oven for about 20 minutes, stirring occasionally, until tender. Transfer to extra-large bowl.

Add tomatoes. Let stand until cool.

Place next 7 ingredients in food processor. Process with on/off motion until finely chopped. With motor running, add second amount of olive oil through hole in feed chute until smooth.

(continued on next page)

Brush both sides of steak with 2 tbsp. (30 mL) basil mixture. Sprinkle with salt and pepper. Place on greased wire rack set on ungreased baking sheet. Broil for about 5 minutes per side until internal temperature reaches 145°F (63°C) for medium-rare or until steak reaches desired doneness. Transfer to cutting board. Cover with foil. Let stand for 10 minutes. Cut diagonally across grain into very thin slices. Cut slices in half crosswise. Add to pepper mixture. Add remaining basil mixture. Toss gently. Makes about 10 cups (2.5 L).

1 1/2 cups (375 mL): 296 Calories; 21.1 g Total Fat (12.9 g Mono, 2.6 g Poly, 4.7 g Sat); 28 mg Cholesterol; 12 g Carbohydrate; 5 g Fibre; 17 g Protein; 256 mg Sodium

Pictured on page 35.

Bruschetta Beef Salad Wrap

Beef, tomatoes, lettuce and cheese are all wrapped up for a satisfying lunch with classic bruschetta flavour! Wrap well and chill until lunchtime. Feel free to use leftover roast beef or deli roast beef.

Diced seeded Roma (plum) tomato	2/3 cup	150 mL
Basil pesto	2 tsp.	10 mL
Mayonnaise	2 tsp.	10 mL
Thinly sliced green onion	2 tsp.	10 mL
Pepper, sprinkle		
Finely chopped cooked roast beef	1/4 cup	60 mL
Grated part-skim mozzarella cheese	2 tbsp.	30 mL
Grated Parmesan cheese	1 tsp.	5 mL
Large green leaf lettuce leaf	1	1
Pesto (or whole-wheat) flour tortilla (9 inch, 22 cm, diameter)	1	1

Combine first 5 ingredients in small bowl.

Add next 3 ingredients. Stir until coated.

Place lettuce on tortilla. Spoon tomato mixture along centre of lettuce. Fold sides over filling. Roll up from bottom to enclose filling. Makes 1 salad wrap.

1 salad wrap: 375 Calories; 20.3 g Total Fat (1.0 g Mono, 1.6 g Poly, 5.9 g Sat); 35 mg Cholesterol; 30 g Carbohydrate; 2 g Fibre; 20 g Protein; 1114 mg Sodium

Tender Beef and Potato Salad

Baby potatoes and beef blend well with colourful peppers, generously dressed in Dijon basil cream.

Thinly sliced green onion	1/2 cup	125 mL
Sour cream	1/4 cup	60 mL
Lemon juice	2 tbsp.	30 mL
Mayonnaise	2 tbsp.	30 mL
Chopped fresh basil	1 1/2 tbsp.	25 mL
Dijon mustard	1 tbsp.	15 mL
Liquid honey	1 tbsp.	15 mL
Salt	1/4 tsp.	1 mL
Pepper	1/8 tsp.	0.5 mL
Red (or white) baby potatoes, halved, larger ones quartered	2 lbs.	900 g
Cooking oil	2 tsp.	10 mL
Salt	1/8 tsp.	0.5 mL
Pepper	1/8 tsp.	0.5 mL
Beef rib-eye steak (about 1/2 inch, 12 mm, thick)	3/4 lb.	340 g
Cooking oil	1 tsp.	5 mL
Salt, sprinkle		
Pepper, sprinkle		
Roasted red peppers, drained and blotted dry, chopped	1/2 cup	125 mL
Thinly sliced celery	1/2 cup	125 mL

Combine first 9 ingredients in large bowl. Chill.

Toss next 4 ingredients in separate large bowl. Arrange in single layer on greased baking sheet with sides. Bake in 400°F (205°C) oven for about 35 minutes until tender and starting to brown. Let stand until cool.

Brush both sides of steak with second amount of cooking oil. Sprinkle with second amounts of salt and pepper. Heat large frying pan on medium-high. Add steak. Cook for 2 to 3 minutes per side until internal temperature reaches 145°F (63°C) for medium-rare or until steak reaches desired doneness. Transfer to cutting board. Let stand until cool. Cut steak across grain into thin slices. Add steak and potato mixture to green onion mixture.

(continued on next page)

Add red pepper and celery. Stir. Chill for 2 hours. Makes about 5 cups (1.25 L).

1 cup (250 mL): 380 Calories; 15.2 g Total Fat (4.0 g Mono, 1.1 g Poly, 4.6 g Sat); 40 mg Cholesterol; 40 g Carbohydrate; 2 g Fibre; 17 g Protein; 471 mg Sodium

Green Bean Panzanella Salad

This green bean salad features chewy bread croutons and Asiago cheese, and has a delightful hint of citrus—a refreshing reminder of summer in a year-round salad.

Fresh (or frozen) whole green beans, halved	4 cups	1 L
Sliced onion	1 1/2 cups	375 mL
Thinly sliced fennel bulb (white part only)	1 1/2 cups	375 mL
Olive oil	1 tbsp.	15 mL
Pepper	1/4 tsp.	1 mL
Olive oil	2 tbsp.	30 mL
Cubed ciabatta bread (3/4 inch, 2 cm, pieces)	3 cups	750 mL
Pine nuts	1/3 cup	75 mL
Olive oil	1/4 cup	60 mL
Red wine vinegar	3 tbsp.	50 mL
Dijon mustard (with whole seeds)	1 tbsp.	15 mL
Grated lemon zest	1 1/2 tsp.	7 mL
Salt	1/4 tsp.	1 mL
Pepper	1/8 tsp.	0.5 mL
Grated Asiago cheese	1/3 cup	75 mL

Toss first 5 ingredients in large bowl. Arrange in single layer on greased baking sheet with sides. Bake in 400°F (205°C) oven for about 20 minutes, stirring once, until vegetables are tender-crisp. Return to same large bowl. Let stand until cool.

Heat second amount of olive oil in large frying pan on medium. Add bread and pine nuts. Heat and stir for about 4 minutes until pine nuts are golden. Add to green bean mixture.

Whisk next 6 ingredients in small bowl. Add to bread mixture. Toss.

Sprinkle with cheese. Makes about 7 cups (1.75 L).

1 cup (250 mL): 285 Calories; 20.8 g Total Fat (11.2 g Mono, 4.2 g Poly, 3.4 g Sat); 5 mg Cholesterol; 23 g Carbohydrate; 5 g Fibre; 6 g Protein; 291 mg Sodium

Slaws & Vegetables

Smoked Salmon Potato Salad

Strike gold with this luxurious potato salad, perfect for a special luncheon.

Peeled yellow-fleshed potatoes, cubed	2 lb.	900 g
Salt	1 tsp.	5 mL
Julienned red pepper	1/2 cup	125 mL
Sour cream	1/2 cup	125 mL
Chopped fresh chives	2 tbsp.	30 mL
(or 1 1/2 tsp., 7 mL, dried)		
Chopped fresh dill	2 tbsp.	30 mL
(or 1 1/2 tsp., 7 mL, dried)		
Lemon juice	2 tbsp.	30 mL
Salt	1/2 tsp.	2 mL
Pepper	1/8 tsp.	0.5 mL
Fresh asparagus, trimmed of tough ends	3/4 lb.	340 g
Salt	1/2 tsp.	2 mL
Ice water		
Butter lettuce leaves	16	16
Smoked salmon slices, cut into strips	4 oz.	113 g
Chopped fresh chives (optional)	1 tbsp.	15 mL

Pour water into large saucepan until about 1 inch (2.5 cm) deep. Add potato and salt. Bring to a boil. Reduce heat to medium. Boil gently, covered, for 12 to 15 minutes until tender. Drain. Rinse with cold water. Drain well. Transfer to large bowl.

Combine next 7 ingredients in small bowl. Add to potato. Stir.

Pour water into large frying pan until about 1 inch (2.5 cm) deep. Bring to a boil. Add asparagus and salt. Reduce heat to medium. Boil gently, covered, for about 4 minutes until tender-crisp. Drain.

Plunge into ice water in medium bowl. Let stand for 10 minutes until cold. Drain.

Arrange lettuce on 4 serving plates. Spoon potato mixture over lettuce. Arrange asparagus and salmon over potato mixture.

Sprinkle with second amount of chives. Serves 4.

1 serving: 321 Calories; 6.8 g Total Fat (0.6 g Mono, 0.6 g Poly, 3.9 g Sat); 27 mg Cholesterol; 53 g Carbohydrate; 7 g Fibre; 13 g Protein; 830 mg Sodium

Pictured on page 143.

Spanish Potato Salad

This attractive, tapas-inspired salad boasts a zesty vegetable medley, with wedges of hard-cooked egg offering a rustic accent. A hearty dish that pairs well with a bold red wine.

Red baby potatoes, quartered	2 lbs.	900 g
Coarsely chopped onion	1/2 cup	125 mL
Olive (or cooking) oil	1 tbsp.	15 mL
Smoked sweet paprika (or chili powder)	1 tsp.	5 mL
Salt	1/2 tsp.	2 mL
Pepper	1/4 tsp.	1 mL
Sun-dried tomato dressing	1/2 cup	125 mL
Smoked sweet paprika (or chili powder)	1/2 tsp.	2 mL
Tomato paste (see Tip, page 76)	1/2 tsp.	2 mL
Dried crushed chilies	1/4 tsp.	1 mL
Garlic clove, minced	1	1
(or 1/4 tsp., 1 mL, powder)		
Chopped tomato	2 cups	500 mL
Chopped green pepper	1 cup	250 mL
Frozen tiny peas, thawed	1 cup	250 mL
Chopped fresh parsley	1 tbsp.	15 mL
(or 3/4 tsp., 4 mL, dried)		
Large hard-cooked eggs, quartered	4	4
Chopped fresh parsley	1 tsp.	5 mL
(or 1/4 tsp., 4 mL, dried)		

Combine first 6 ingredients in large bowl. Arrange in single layer on greased baking sheet with sides. Bake in 400°F (205°C) oven for about 30 minutes, stirring at halftime, until potato is tender and starting to brown. Return to same large bowl. Let stand until cool.

Combine next 5 ingredients in small bowl. Add to potato.

Add next 4 ingredients. Toss.

Arrange egg wedges around potato mixture. Sprinkle with second amount of parsley. Serves 6.

1 serving: 283 Calories; 9.6 g Total Fat (3.1 g Mono, 0.9 g Poly, 1.8 g Sat); 141 mg Cholesterol; 39 g Carbohydrate; 5 g Fibre; 10 g Protein; 517 mg Sodium

Pictured on page 144.

Mango Jicama Slaw

This fresh combination of crunchy cucumber and jicama (HEE-kah-mah), rich cottage cheese and sweet mango is a perfect meal salad to serve up for lunch.

Grated peeled jicama	4 cups	1 L
2% cottage cheese	1 1/2 cups	375 mL
Finely diced seeded English cucumber (with peel)	1 1/2 cups	375 mL
Finely chopped ripe mango	3/4 cup	175 mL
MANGO LIME DRESSING		
Olive (or cooking) oil	1/2 cup	125 mL
Chopped ripe mango	1/4 cup	60 mL
Lime juice	1/4 cup	60 mL
Liquid honey	1 tbsp.	15 mL
Salt	1/4 tsp.	1 mL
Pepper	1/4 tsp.	1 mL

Combine first 4 ingredients in large bowl.

Mango Lime Dressing: Process all 6 ingredients in blender or food processor until smooth. Makes about 1 cup (250 mL). Add to jicama mixture. Stir. Makes about 6 cups (1.5 L).

1 cup (250 mL): 280 Calories; 20.0 g Total Fat (13.7 g Mono, 2.8 g Poly, 3.4 g Sat); 5 mg Cholesterol; 19 g Carbohydrate; 5 g Fibre; 9 g Protein; 331 mg Sodium

1. Peppy Salad Pizza, page 124
2. Layered Paella Salad, page 128
3. Smoked Salmon Potato Salad, page 140

Props: Maxwell Williams
         Jars

Avocado Potato Salad

Potato salad is no longer just for picnics! Before being dressed in a creamy avocado and ranch blend, these potatoes are roasted in the oven—perfect for when it's too cold out to use the barbecue.

Red baby potatoes, quartered	2 lbs.	900 g
Cooking oil	2 tbsp.	30 mL
Montreal steak spice	1 tbsp.	15 mL
Chopped avocado	1 cup	250 mL
Ranch dressing	1/2 cup	125 mL
Chopped fresh cilantro (or parsley)	2 tbsp.	30 mL
Can of kernel corn	12 oz.	341 mL
Diced English cucumber (with peel)	1 cup	250 mL
Diced red pepper	1 cup	250 mL
Real bacon bits	1/4 cup	60 mL

Combine first 3 ingredients in large bowl. Arrange in single layer on greased baking sheet with sides. Cook in 450°F (230°C) oven for about 20 minutes until potatoes are tender. Return to same large bowl. Cool.

Process next 3 ingredients in blender or food processor until smooth. Add to potato mixture.

Add remaining 4 ingredients. Stir. Makes about 7 cups (1.75 mL).

1 cup (250 mL): 326 Calories; 16.9 g Total Fat (4.8 g Mono, 1.7 g Poly, 2.4 g Sat); 8 mg Cholesterol; 37 g Carbohydrate; 5 g Fibre; 7 g Protein; 704 mg Sodium

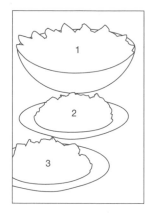

1. Spanish Potato Salad, page 141
2. Roasted Roots and Turkey, page 148
3. Two-Potato Black Bean Salad, page 146

Props: Studio Nova
       Leonardo Da Vinci

Two-Potato Black Bean Salad

South American-inspired flavours united by a spicy citrus vinaigrette—a tasty answer to "What's for lunch?"

Cubed fresh peeled orange-fleshed sweet potato (1 inch, 2.5 cm, pieces)	3 cups	750 mL
Cubed peeled potato (1 inch, 2.5 cm, pieces)	1 1/2 cups	375 mL
Chopped red pepper (1 inch, 2.5 cm, pieces)	1 cup	250 mL
Cooking oil	1 tbsp.	15 mL
Salt	1/4 tsp.	1 mL
Pepper	1/4 tsp.	1 mL
Can of black beans, rinsed and drained	19 oz.	540 mL
Thinly sliced red onion	1/4 cup	60 mL
Chopped fresh cilantro (or parsley)	2 tbsp.	30 mL

CHIPOTLE LIME VINAIGRETTE

Olive (or cooking) oil	1/4 cup	60 mL
Lime juice	2 tbsp.	30 mL
Red wine vinegar	1 tbsp.	15 mL
Finely chopped chipotle peppers in adobo sauce (see Tip, page 147)	1 tsp.	5 mL
Granulated sugar	1 tsp.	5 mL
Salt	1/2 tsp.	2 mL
Grated lime zest	1/4 tsp.	1 mL
Small garlic clove, minced (or 1/8 tsp., 0.5 mL, powder)	1	1

Combine first 6 ingredients in large bowl. Arrange in single layer on greased baking sheet with sides. Bake in 375°F (190°C) oven for about 30 minutes until tender. Return to same large bowl. Cool.

Add next 3 ingredients.

Chipotle Lime Vinaigrette: Whisk all 8 ingredients in small bowl. Makes about 1/2 cup (125 mL). Drizzle over potato mixture. Toss. Makes about 6 cups (1.5 L).

1 cup (250 mL): 281 Calories; 12.5 g Total Fat (8.0 g Mono, 2.8 g Poly, 1.5 g Sat); 0 mg Cholesterol; 37 g Carbohydrate; 8 g Fibre; 7 g Protein; 610 mg Sodium

Pictured on page 144.

Blue-Ribbon Potato Salad

A blue ribbon-worthy addition to your next picnic or potluck, classic potato salad goes upscale with European cheese, smoky ham and toasty pecans. Garnish with chopped fresh parsley and sliced radish.

Peeled waxy potatoes, cubed	2 lbs.	900 g
Salt	1 tsp.	5 mL
Diced Black Forest ham	1 1/4 cups	300 mL
Diced Gruyère cheese	1 cup	250 mL
Diced celery	1/2 cup	125 mL
Diced red onion	1/2 cup	125 mL
Pecan halves, toasted (see Tip, page 134)	1/2 cup	125 mL
Large hard-cooked eggs, chopped	2	2
Mayonnaise	2/3 cup	150 mL
Sweet pickle relish	3 tbsp.	50 mL
White wine vinegar	1 tbsp.	15 mL
Honey Dijon mustard	1 tsp.	5 mL
Salt	1/4 tsp.	1 mL
Pepper	1/8 tsp.	0.5 mL

Pour water into large saucepan until about 1 inch (2.5 cm) deep. Add potato and salt. Bring to a boil. Reduce heat to medium. Boil gently, covered, for 12 to 15 minutes until tender. Drain. Rinse with cold water. Drain well. Transfer to large bowl.

Add next 6 ingredients.

Combine remaining 6 ingredients in small bowl. Add to potato mixture. Stir gently to coat. Makes about 8 cups (2 L).

1 cup (250 mL): 423 Calories; 28.5 g Total Fat (5.9 g Mono, 2.2 g Poly, 6.7 g Sat); 98 mg Cholesterol; 27 g Carbohydrate; 3 g Fibre; 15 g Protein; 301 mg Sodium

 tip   Chipotle chili peppers are smoked jalapeno peppers. Be sure to wash your hands after handling. To store any leftover chipotle peppers, divide into recipe-friendly portions and freeze, with sauce, in airtight containers for up to one year.

Roasted Roots and Turkey

A great way to use leftover turkey and cranberry sauce after a holiday meal!
A delicate dressing complements roasted root vegetables and tender turkey.

Baby potatoes, quartered	1 1/2 lbs.	680 g
Chopped carrot (1/2 inch, 12 mm, pieces)	1 1/2 cups	375 mL
Chopped parsnip (1/2 inch, 12 mm, pieces)	1 cup	250 mL
Chopped yellow turnip (rutabaga), 1/2 inch (12 mm) pieces	1 cup	250 mL
Olive (or cooking) oil	2 tbsp.	30 mL
Chopped fresh rosemary (or 1/2 tsp., 2 mL, dried)	2 tsp.	10 mL
Garlic clove, minced (or 1/4 tsp., 1 mL, powder)	1	1
Salt	1/2 tsp.	2 mL
Chopped cooked turkey	2 cups	500 mL
Diced celery	1/2 cup	125 mL
Dried cranberries	1/2 cup	125 mL
Chopped sweet onion	3 tbsp.	50 mL
Olive (or cooking) oil	3 tbsp.	50 mL
White wine vinegar	4 tsp.	20 mL
Whole (or jellied) cranberry sauce	4 tsp.	20 mL
Dry mustard	1 1/2 tsp.	7 mL
Salt	1/4 tsp.	1 mL
Pepper	1/4 tsp.	1 mL
Chopped fresh parsley (or flakes), for garnish		

Combine first 8 ingredients in large bowl. Arrange in single layer on greased baking sheet with sides. Bake in 450°F (230°C) oven for about 30 minutes until tender and starting to brown. Return to large bowl. Let stand until cool.

Add next 3 ingredients.

Process next 7 ingredients in blender or food processor until smooth. Add to potato mixture. Stir. Sprinkle with parsley. Makes about 8 cups (2 L).

1 cup (250 mL): 257 Calories; 9.9 g Total Fat (6.5 g Mono, 1.6 g Poly, 1.6 g Sat); 34 mg Cholesterol; 30 g Carbohydrate; 4 g Fibre; 13 g Protein; 314 mg Sodium

Pictured on page 144.

Tangy Potato Salad

This warm meal salad is reminiscent of German potato salad with smoky bacon and a tangy, cooked dressing, but we've added toasty walnuts and crumbled blue cheese to the mix.

White baby potatoes, quartered	2 lbs.	900 g
Salt	1 tsp.	5 mL
Coarsely chopped walnut pieces	2/3 cup	150 mL
Bacon slices, diced	8	8
Sliced green onion	1/4 cup	60 mL
Apple cider vinegar	3 tbsp.	50 mL
Red wine vinegar	3 tbsp.	50 mL
Dry mustard	1 tsp.	5 mL
Paprika	1 tsp.	5 mL
Granulated sugar	1/2 tsp.	2 mL
Crumbled blue cheese	1/3 cup	75 mL

Pour water into large saucepan until about 1 inch (2.5 cm) deep. Add potato and salt. Bring to a boil. Reduce heat to medium. Boil gently, covered, for 12 to 15 minutes until tender. Drain. Transfer to large bowl. Let stand for 30 minutes.

Combine walnuts and bacon in large frying pan on medium. Cook for about 8 minutes, stirring occasionally, until bacon is crisp. Transfer with slotted spoon to paper towel-lined plate to drain. Drain and discard all but 2 tbsp. (30 mL) bacon drippings from pan.

Add next 6 ingredients. Heat and stir, scraping any brown bits from bottom of pan, until boiling. Remove from heat.

Add blue cheese and green onion mixture to potato. Toss. Scatter bacon and walnuts over top. Makes about 6 cups (1.5 L).

1 cup (250 mL): 327 Calories; 18.8 g Total Fat (5.3 g Mono, 7.3 g Poly, 5.1 g Sat); 19 mg Cholesterol; 30 g Carbohydrate; 3 g Fibre; 10 g Protein; 345 mg Sodium

---

Paré Pointer

My dog is pretty dirty, but he's even prettier when he's clean.

Sausage Cabbage Salad

Sausages are right at home with shredded cabbage in this fresh, crunchy salad topped with tasty garlic croutons.

GARLIC CROUTONS		
Butter (or hard margarine), melted	2 tbsp.	30 mL
Garlic salt	1/4 tsp.	1 mL
White bread cubes (1/2 inch 12 mm, pieces)	1 1/2 cups	375 mL

SALAD		
Pork breakfast sausages	4	4
Shredded cabbage, lightly packed	4 cups	1 L
Chopped green pepper	1 cup	250 mL
Chopped celery	1/2 cup	125 mL
Chopped green onion	1/4 cup	60 mL

BACON DRESSING		
Bacon slices, diced	4	4
All-purpose flour	2 tsp.	10 mL
Water	1/2 cup	125 mL
Apple cider vinegar	2 tbsp.	30 mL
Granulated sugar	1 tbsp.	15 mL
Pepper	1/8 tsp.	0.5 mL
Egg yolk (large), see Safety Tip 1, next page	1	1

Garlic Croutons: Combine butter and garlic salt in large bowl. Add bread cubes. Toss until coated. Arrange in single layer on greased baking sheet with sides. Bake in 375°F (190°C) oven for about 15 minutes, turning once, until crisp and golden. Let stand until cool. Makes about 1 1/2 cups (375 mL).

Salad: Cook sausages in medium frying pan on medium for about 15 minutes, turning occasionally, until no longer pink inside. Transfer to paper towel-lined plate to drain. Transfer to cutting board. Cut diagonally into 1/4 inch (6 mm) slices. Transfer to separate large bowl.

Add next 4 ingredients. Toss.

(continued on next page)

Bacon Dressing: Wipe same frying pan with paper towels. Add bacon. Cook on medium, stirring occasionally, until crisp. Transfer with slotted spoon to paper towel-lined plate to drain. Drain and discard all but 1 tbsp. (15 mL) drippings.

Add flour. Heat and stir for 1 minute. Slowly add water, stirring constantly until smooth. Add next 3 ingredients. Heat and stir for 2 to 3 minutes until boiling and thickened. Remove from heat. Let stand for 5 minutes to cool slightly. Transfer to blender.

Add bacon and egg yolk. Carefully process until almost smooth (see Safety Tip 2). Makes about 3/4 cup (175 mL). Drizzle over Salad. Toss. Scatter Garlic Croutons over top. Makes about 7 cups (1.75 L).

1 cup (250 mL): 143 Calories; 9.7 g Total Fat (3.6 g Mono, 1.0 g Poly, 4.3 g Sat); 50 mg Cholesterol; 10 g Carbohydrate; 2 g Fibre; 5 g Protein; 267 mg Sodium

Safety Tip 1: This recipe contains uncooked egg. Make sure to use fresh, clean Grade A eggs. Keep chilled and consume the same day the recipe is prepared. Always discard leftovers. Pregnant women, young children and the elderly are not advised to eat anything containing raw egg.

Safety Tip 2: Follow manufacturer's instructions for processing hot liquids.

Paré Pointer

That boy must be a ladder - he has a stepfather.

Measurement Tables

Throughout this book measurements are given in Conventional and Metric measure. To compensate for differences between the two measurements due to rounding, a full metric measure is not always used. The cup used is the standard 8 fluid ounce. Temperature is given in degrees Fahrenheit and Celsius. Baking pan measurements are in inches and centimetres as well as quarts and litres. An exact metric conversion is given below as well as the working equivalent (Metric Standard Measure).

Spoons

Conventional Measure	Metric Exact Conversion Millilitre (mL)	Metric Standard Measure Millilitre (mL)
1/8 teaspoon (tsp.)	0.6 mL	0.5 mL
1/4 teaspoon (tsp.)	1.2 mL	1, mL
1/2 teaspoon (tsp.)	2.4 mL	2 mL
1 teaspoon (tsp.)	4.7 mL	5 mL
2 teaspoons (tsp.)	9.4 mL	10 mL
1 tablespoon (tbsp.)	14.2 mL	15 mL

Cups

Conventional Measure	Metric Exact Conversion Millilitre (mL)	Metric Standard Measure Millilitre (mL)
1/4 cup (4 tbsp.)	56.8 mL	60 mL
1/3 cup (5 1/3 tbsp.)	75.6 mL	75 mL
1/2 cup (8 tbsp.)	113.7 mL	125 mL
2/3 cup (10 2/3 tbsp.)	151.2 mL	150 mL
3/4 cup (12 tbsp.)	170.5 mL	175 mL
1 cup (16 tbsp.)	227.3 mL	250 mL
4 1/2 cups	1022.9 mL	1000 mL (1 L)

Oven Temperatures

Fahrenheit (°F)	Celsius (°C)
175°	80°
200°	95°
225°	110°
250°	120°
275°	140°
300°	150°
325°	160°
350°	175°
375°	190°
400°	205°
425°	220°
450°	230°
475°	240°
500°	260°

Dry Measurements

Conventional Measure Ounces (oz.)	Metric Exact Conversion Grams (g)	Metric Standard Measure Grams (g)
1 oz.	28.3 g	28 g
2 oz.	56.7 g	57 g
3 oz.	85.0 g	85 g
4 oz.	113.4 g	125 g
5 oz.	141.7 g	140 g
6 oz.	170.1 g	170 g
7 oz.	198.4 g	200 g
8 oz.	226.8 g	250 g
16 oz.	453.6 g	500 g
32 oz.	907.2 g	1000 g (1 kg)

Pans

Conventional Inches	Metric Centimetres
8x8 inch	20x20 cm
9x9 inch	22x22 cm
9x13 inch	22x33 cm
10x15 inch	25x38 cm
11x17 inch	28x43 cm
8x2 inch round	20x5 cm
9x2 inch round	22x5 cm
10x4 1/2 inch tube	25x11 cm
8x4x3 inch loaf	20x10x7.5 cm
9x5x3 inch loaf	22x12.5x7.5 cm

Casseroles

CANADA & BRITAIN Standard Size Casserole	Exact Metric Measure	UNITED STATES Standard Size Casserole	Exact Metric Measure
1 qt. (5 cups)	1.13 L	1 qt. (4 cups)	900 mL
1 1/2 qts. (7 1/2 cups)	1.69 L	1 1/2 qts. (6 cups)	1.35 L
2 qts. (10 cups)	2.25 L	2 qts. (8 cups)	1.8 L
2 1/2 qts. (12 1/2 cups)	2.81 L	2 1/2 qts. (10 cups)	2.25 L
3 qts. (15 cups)	3.38 L	3 qts. (12 cups)	2.7 L
4 qts. (20 cups)	4.5 L	4 qts. (16 cups)	3.6 L
5 qts. (25 cups)	5.63 L	5 qts. (20 cups)	4.5 L

Recipe Index

153

154

155

157

Complete your Original Series Collection!

- ❏ 150 Delicious Squares
- ❏ Appetizers
- ❏ Cookies
- ❏ Barbecues
- ❏ Preserves
- ❏ Slow Cooker Recipes
- ❏ Stir-Fry
- ❏ Stews, Chilies & Chowders
- ❏ Fondues
- ❏ The Rookie Cook
- ❏ Sweet Cravings
- ❏ Year-Round Grilling
- ❏ Garden Greens
- ❏ Chinese Cooking
- ❏ The Beverage Book
- ❏ Slow Cooker Dinners
- ❏ 30-Minute Weekday Meals
- ❏ Potluck Dishes
- ❏ Ground Beef Recipes
- ❏ 4-Ingredient Recipes
- ❏ Kids' Healthy Cooking
- ❏ Mostly Muffins
- ❏ Soups
- ❏ Simple Suppers
- ❏ Diabetic Cooking
- ❏ Chicken Now
- ❏ Kids Do Snacks
- ❏ Low-Fat Express
- ❏ Choosing Sides
- ❏ Perfect Pasta & Sauces
- ❏ 30-Minute Diabetic Cooking
- ❏ Healthy In A Hurry
- ❏ Table For Two
- ❏ Catch Of The Day
- ❏ Kids Do Baking
- ❏ 5-Ingredient Slow Cooker Recipes
- ❏ Diabetic Dinners
- ❏ Easy Healthy Recipes
- ❏ 30-Minute Pantry
- ❏ Everyday Barbecuing
- ❏ Meal Salads
- ❏ Healthy Slow Cooker
- ❏ Breads
- ❏ Anytime Casseroles
- ❏ Asian Cooking
  NEW April 1/11

Company's Coming News Bite Sign up

FREE Online NEWSLETTER

Subscribe to our **free** News Bite newsletter and get the following benefits:

- **Special** offers & promotions
- **FREE** recipes & cooking tips
- **Previews** of new and upcoming titles
- **Automatic** entry to exciting contests
- **Ability** to purchase new titles before they reach store shelves

Subscribe today!

www.companyscoming.com
visit our website

Each Focus Series book is a mini feature event—priced to make collecting them all especially easy.

Focus Series

- ❏ Apple Appeal
- ❏ Berries & Cream
- ❏ Carrot Craze
- ❏ Chicken Breast Finesse
- ❏ Chilled Thrills
- ❏ Chocolate Squared
- ❏ Coffee Cake Classics
- ❏ Cookie Jar Classics
- ❏ Cranberrys Cravings
- ❏ Dip, Dunk & Dab
- ❏ Easy Roasting
- ❏ Fab Finger Food
- ❏ Fruit Squared
- ❏ Hearty Soups
- ❏ Hot Bites
- ❏ Lemon Lime Zingers
- ❏ Mushroom Magic
- ❏ Salads To Go
- ❏ Shrimp Delicious
- ❏ Simmering Stews
- ❏ Simply Vegetarian
- ❏ Sips
- ❏ Skewered
- ❏ So Strawberry
- ❏ Splendid Spuds
- ❏ Steak Sizzle
- ❏ Sweet Dreams
- ❏ That's A Wrap
- ❏ Tomato Temptations
- ❏ Tossed
- ❏ Warm Desserts
- ❏ Zucchini Zone